2020

Wish

MW00642071

Best Days

Always

Mark Keys

My
BEST
DAY

PRO BASEBALL I

A collection of best day responses from
former and current players and coaches

MARK KEYS

H-949-645-8109 C-949-531-1373

M K
C E
C Y
O S
O
L
PRESS

1

For Lou Gehrig, one of my favorite baseball players since I was a kid.

INTRODUCTION

In May 1991, I injured my back while working and was placed on permanent disability. Prior to my first back surgery, I had my photo taken with Magic Johnson of the Los Angeles Lakers. Later, Blain Skinner, a friend of mine, was able to get Magic to autograph the snapshot. It made my day.

As a hobby, I began writing to other celebrities asking for autographed photos. Their positive responses amazed me. One weekend while in Palm Springs, California, I met Nat Kipner, an entrepreneur, who suggested I expand my hobby to include famous people from all walks of life. This idea was a godsend. During the next several years, while incapacitated with several more back surgeries and an ankle reconstruction, I collected even more autographs.

One day while out walking, I noticed the magnificent beauty of the simple blue sky. Upon returning home, I thought about what a good day it was, despite my back problems. I felt great! Then it struck me: I wondered what all those people I had been receiving autographs from felt was their "best day."

I began writing letters asking that question. Joey Bishop was the first to reply, and that's how it all began.

McCool Keys Press
5308 Whipville
Newport Beach, CA 92663

Individual Sales, this book is available through most bookstores or can be ordered directly from McCool Keys Press at the address above.

Quantity Sales. Special discounts are available on quantity purchases by corporations, associations, and others. For details, contact the "Special Sales Department" at the publisher's address above.

Printed in the United States of America.

Cover design: Escher Creative eschercreative@sbcglobal.net
949-400-5987

Library of Congress Cataloging-in-Publication Data is available from the publisher.

ISBN 978-0-9897878-8-8

4

ACKNOWLEDGEMENTS:

Dedicated in the memory David "Bucko" Shaw, who always made me laugh, & who I miss everyday

Thank you to all those who were supportive and encouraging to my project:

Rick John, Mike Wilsey and family, John Hamilton and Diane, Cassavete Winstead, The McCarthy Family, Frank Venclick and his parents Frank & Betty, Pat Millican, Jim & Cathie Helfrich, Mary Claire Helfrich and the entire Helfrich Family, Steve Foley, Joe Rogers and family, Jon Sweek, Janet Curci, Mark & Leslie Louvier, Laurie Weddington-Tagg, Heather Hendrickson and her mom, Marilyn, Lora Mulligan, Steve Kalatschan, Kevin & Tess Doody, Dave Roum, Brad Leggett, Chris Rock, Ron Lamerton & family, my "brothers" Fraser and Chris Keys, and my fantastic graphic designer, Erik Escher. A big thank you to Aunt Joan Parker, your help is immeasurable.

A big thank you to all of my doctors over the years: Gausewitz, Safman & Naomi Porter. Rhei, Gerkin, Bae, Hunt, Quist, O'Carroll and Gladys Mendoza, Carlson & Katie, Bruss, Yaru, Dobkin, Gordon, Shukla, Stringer, Wynn, Feinberg, Aly Sheets.

As always, thank you to my wife Laurie. She has been there for me, especially after I got hurt and she has been involved with my project every step of the way. Thanks to my mom, Virginia and mom-in-law Glenell. To my wonderful daughters, Megan & Page— I love you with all of my heart.

Also by Mark Keys

My BEST DAY
SERIES

AS SEEN ON **ESPN**

https://www.espn.com/video/clip/_/id/11924279

 Mybestday_MK   mybestdaybyMarkKeys   markkeys0405

McCool Keys Press · Newport Beach

FOREWARD

A good day, a bad day, and a great day…such is the makeup of our lives. Mark Keys has had them all but manages to live the good days and the best days almost every day. This is a tribute to the love he shares with his family and the courage he shares with us all.

My Best Day is a wonderfully unique insight into what various sports personalities believe defines the highlight of their careers and sometimes even their lives. We all have great days and we all have memorable days…and then we have our "best day" and that is the moment that sits in our memory forever. It is that day that we greedily recall with anticipation and wonder. The days chronicled here will help you recall your own "Best Day."

-FRED LYNN

My Best Day was when Mr. George Sisler, General Manager of the Rochester Red Wings (International League) waited at the ballpark while our team was returning from a series in Toronto, Canada by bus. Ticket in hand to tell me I was going to the Big Leagues the next day- June 1958! Saint Louis Cardinals, the team that signed me in 1954.

There isn't a most memorable day than my first day in the Major Leagues in June 1958. I was called up from Rochester 3A (International League). After putting on my uniform, I am walking out towards the playing field-the locker near the exit first locker out of the club house in St. Louis old Busch Stadium was Stan Musial's. My uniform pants were a little too big –size 38- he called me over and introduced himself and welcomed my venture into the Big Leagues and at the same time he called Butch Yakeman, the little club house manager for St. Louis, and told him, " Butch give Ruben a pair of pants that fit him, will you."

-RUBEN AMARO SR
Shortstop, St. Louis Cardinals, Philadelphia Phillies, NY Yankees, California Angels,1964 Golden Glove, Mexican Hall of Fame, Major League Baseball Hall of Fame

My Best Day was winning the 1981 World Championship

-KEN LANDREAUX

Center Fielder: CA Angels, Minnesota Twins, LA Dodgers,
1981 World Series Champion (Dodgers), 1X All-Star

My Best Day in Baseball? My 1st hit in the Major Leagues was a home run off Dave "Boo" Ferriss of the Boston Red Sox—I thought nothing could be better than breaking in the Big Leagues like that, Great Day!

-DICK ADAMS

First Baseman, Philadelphia A's 1947

I have three Best Days- when each of my children were born.

-MATT KEOUGH

Pitcher, Oakland A, St. Louis Cardinals, NY Yankees, 1978 All-Star

My Best Day was in June of 1975, I went 5-6 with three home runs, one triple, one single and ten RBI's. The only out I made was a line out to second. We won 15-1.

-FRED LYNN

Center Field; Boston Red Sox, Anaheim Angels, Baltimore Orioles, Detroit Tigers, San Diego Padres, 9X All-Star, 1975 Rookie of the Year and AL MVP, 4X Golden Glover, Boston Red Sox Hall of Fame

My Best Day was when I had my siblings Toby & Thomas and my two daughters, Haley & Katie all together with my wife, Jan, on Family Day in Texas 1994.

-TOBY HARRAH

Third Baseman, Texas Rangers, NY Yankees, 4X All-Star, Texas Ranger Hall of Fame, Coach: Colorado Rockies

My Best Day was probably when I got called up to the Majors, May 5, 2014. I had been working so hard my whole life and I achieved my dream. My dad would have been so proud; he passed away in 2012. We were like peas & carrots-we were so close.

-CHASE ANDERSON

Pitcher, Arizona Diamond Backs, Milwaukee Brewers

The Best Day of my life was when our 1st child (David) was born October 31, 1964.

-STEVE BLASS
Pitcher, Pittsburg Pirates, 1971 World Series (Pirates), 1972 All-Star

My Best Day was the day I found out my first child was going to be a boy.

-LONNIE CHISENHALL
Third Baseman, Cleveland Indians

My Best Day is every day I can see the Big Light in the sky.

Baseball Best Day was when I finally walked onto the field at Fenway Park, September of 1970.

-BOB MONTGOMERY

Catcher, Boston Red Sox, Famous for being the last MLB player to bat without a helmet

The best game I had emotionally was my first no-hitter of my career for the Reds against the Cardinals June 16th, 1978. Prior to that, I had three no-hitters going into the 9th inning that were spoiled with a hit. It was a fantastic feeling and a great day personally.

-TOM SEAVER

Pitcher, New York Mets, Cincinnati Reds, Boston Red Sox, 12X All-Star, 3X NL Cy Young Winner, 1969 World Series Champion (Mets)

When I pitched in the 1981 World Series

-FERNANDO VALENZUELA

Pitcher, LA Dodgers, Angels, Orioles, 6X All-Star, 1981 World Series
Champion (Dodgers), 1990 No Hitter

I have had a lot of Best Days-the very Best Day was 3 hits at
Fenway Park in Boston in 1940.

-CARL MILES

(as told by his wife Norma Miles)
Pitcher, Philadelphia Athletics

I have had two special days in my baseball career. My first Major League base hit July 5, 1940 and when I was a coach with the Pittsburg Pirates, 1979. The Pirates were World Champions "We Are Family"

-AL MONCHAK

Shortstop, Philadelphia Phillies, 2009 Roland Hemond Award for Baseball development contribution

My Best Day was July 11, 2008 when I nearly pitched a complete came shutout at LA in my 1st Major League start... Eight and two /thirds innings and then a run scored against me. Closer Kevin Gregg got the final out and the Marlins and I won the game 3-1.

-CHRIS VOLSTED

Pitcher, Florida Marlins, Chicago Cubs, Pittsburg Pirates, Chicago White Sox

I would have to say the Best Day for me was being in the starting lineup in 1952. We played the Senators and I caught the Presidents' (Harry S. Truman) ball and was introduced to him with a handshake.

-TED LEPCIO

Utility Infielder, Boston Red Sox, Florida Marlins, Chicago Cubs, Pittsburg Pirates

Being able to look up in the stands and see my parents when I went up to bat in my second Major League Baseball game ever.

-JORDAN PACHECO
First Base/Catcher, Colorado Rockies, Arizona Diamond Backs, Cincinnati Reds

I guess my Best Day, at least most memorable, was catching the no-hitter thrown by Jim Bibby against the Oakland A's in 1973. Also, the last game at RFK Stadium in Washington DC was forfeited against the Yankees in 1971.

-RICH BILLINGS

Left Field/Catcher, Washington Senators, Texas Rangers, St. Louis Cardinals

Probably "My Best Day" in baseball would be the moment that David Freese hit the walk-off homer in game 6 of the 2011 World Series. I was with my family and was able to enjoy the moment in all its glory.

-WILLIAM O. DeWITT III

President St Louis Cardinals, 2006 & 2011 World Series Champions (Cardinals)

Buying my parents, a home was the happiest moment of my life! Not winning batting titles, not winning championships, but doing this for my parents was the best. I don't have to worry about them, and they never have to work again.

-LOU GEHRIG

First Base; New York Yankees, 7X All-Star, 6X World Series Champion (Yankees), 2X AL MVP, 3X Homerun leader, 5X RBI leader, June 3, 1932 hit 4 homeruns in one game, Major League Baseball All-Century Team, National Baseball Hall of Fame

It was the bottom of 11th inning on September 23, 1957 and I hit a homerun to win the pennant. I hit the homerun, and low and behold, I looked at home plate, every one of my teammates were there to greet me. Hitting that homerun was one of the greatest thrills in my whole life.

-HANK AARON

Right Field; Milwaukee / Atlanta Braves, Milwaukee Brewers, 25X All-Star, 1957 World Series Champion (Brewers) 1957 National 3X Golden Glove Award, NL MVP 1957, 4X NL Homerun leader, 4X NL RBI leader, Atlanta Braves Hall of Fame & #44 retired, Major League Baseball All-Century Team, National Baseball Hall of Fame

On the first day of the 1951 season I won my 30th win-that was my Best Day.

-NED GARBER

Pitcher, Cleveland Indians, Detroit Tigers, KC Athletics, LA Angels, 1951 All-Star

During my 56-game hitting streak, I spent a lot of time having dinner with Jerry Spatola and his family. His wife, Rose, made great Italian dinners. Jerry's daughters were there, and sometime the Spatola cousins, along with other friends. Great food, wine and happy commotion was very relaxing to me. The dinners at the Spatolas reminded me of the Best Days as a kid growing up with my family in San Francisco.

-JOE DiMAGGIO

Center Field; New York Yankees, 13X All-Star, 9X World Series Champion (Yankees), 3X AL MVP, 2X AL Batting Champion. 2X AL Homerun leader, 2X RBI leader, MLB record 56-game hitting streak, New York Yankee #5 retired, Major League Baseball All-Century Team, National Baseball Hall of Fame

My Best Day was when I put the Big League uniform on for the first time, what a big thrill to make a Major League team and make your first start at 18 years old. My hero as a kid growing up in Northern California was Willie Mays, the first time I faced him I almost called a time out to go to the plate and shake his hand; and he hit a home run, The next time in June, 1976, I had the good fortune of striking him out four times in the same game, Biggest Thrill.

-GARY NOLAN

Pitcher, Cincinnati Reds, CA Angels, 1X All-Star,
2X World Series Champion (Reds)

Shut out in World Series history; allowed 6 hits. In 1946 I was the leading pitcher of the American League, 25-6 record. I nosed out two of the greatest, Bob Feller and Hal Newhouser. I had some big wins, but the World Series win was the best one of all. I am truly thankful for the wonderful day and game.

-DAVE "BOO" FERRISS

Pitcher, Boston Red Sox, 1946 All-Star

My father played professional baseball eleven years and was a teammate of Hall of Famer Ty Cobb. (1st player selected in the Hall of Fame) in Detroit 1911. No one, ever, loved the game more than my father. He taught me as much as he could about the game but never once did, I feel pressured to pursue baseball as a career. But, I knew, nevertheless, how proud he would be if I did. So, the best day of my life was when I walked out onto the Major League Ballpark (Crosley Field) of the Cincinnati Reds in April 1947 in a Major League uniform and knew it was also the Best Day for my father.

-EVERETT BUDDY LIVELY

Pitcher, Cincinnati Reds

I started a game for the Pueblo Dodgers (Western League) in 1947. I was not having much luck getting the other team out, so our manager, Walt Alston, who later became the LA Dodgers Manager, took me out of the game. That's when the best day happened. The friend I was supposed to be meeting after the game introduced me to the prettiest girl I have ever seen.

I knew right then; she was the girl I was going to marry. We were married the next year, (1948). This year, we will celebrate our 65th anniversary. Now you know why, that was the best day of my life, when I was first introduced to that pretty girl.

-OMAR "TURK" LOWN

Pitcher, Chicago Cubs, Cincinnati Red Legs, Chicago White Sox, 1959 World Series (White Sox)

My Major League debuts in Toronto; June 18th. Being from Michigan, it was easy for my family and friends to drive to the game and be there to celebrate this event with me. We also ended up winning the game 4-2 and I was credited with the "W" after pitching into the 7th inning.

-SCOTT KAMIENIECKI

Pitcher, NY Yankees, Baltimore Orioles, Cleveland Indians, Atlanta Braves

Wrigley Field, Chicago, opening day April 17, 1947, my first day on the job. I had my first Major League hit on this day; the pitcher was Hank Borowy.

Twice on my way up the ladder they tried to make me quit. My response to that, Gentlemen, if you think you're going to make me quit, I have words of romance for you, "go get intercourse."

-WALLY WESTLAKE

Outfield, Pittsburg Pirates, Cincinnati Reds, Philadelphia Phillies, 1951 All-Star

I played against all these ball players and they were great.

-JIM RIVERA

Outfield, St Louis Browns, Chicago White Sox, Kansas City Athletics,
1955 AL stolen base record

Chicago World Series- 1932. The game I pointed to center field, I called the shot that I was going to hit a home run in the 5th inning of game 3. It was my 10th, and final World Series Championship

-BABE RUTH- As told in a film clip, TCM

Pitcher / Outfield, Boston Red Sox, New York Yankees, Atlanta Braves, 2X All-Star, 7X World Series Champion (3 Red Sox & 4 Yankees), 12X AL Home Run Leader, MLB Hall of Fame

My life is a Best Day. I was lucky at times and excelled when needed- I am very thankful.

-GOOSE GOSSAGE

Pitcher, Chicago White Sox, NY Yankees, San Diego Padres, San Francisco Giants, 9X All-Star, 1978 World Series Champion (Yankees), National Baseball Hall of Fame

My Best Day is when I wake each day. My wife and I are both 94 years old, having married at age 19 in 1941. We have had 75 years together and counting. My baseball career was important, 10 years in the majors, but our commitment to each other stand out as a family.

My Best Day in baseball was July 4th, 1951 in Yankee Stadium where the Nationals beat the Yankees in back-to-back games. In the first game I hit a second 3-run homer in the ninth inning; and in the 2nd game I scored the tie breaking, and game winning run in the eighth inning off Joe Page. Too bad there were not more of them. I also homered the next night with Ed Yost on base, but we lost that one 4-3 against Bob Kasawa. I turn 91 next month, (2013) and God has been my belief since my baptism in 1928.

-GIL COAN

Outfielder, Washington Senators, Baltimore Orioles, Chicago White Sox, New York Giants

My Best Day was actually a three-day period in April 1981. The first day was Sunday, April 26th. It was the final game of a three-game series against the Boston Red Sox at Memorial Stadium in Baltimore. In the first inning I hit a three-run homer off Dennis Eckersley. I followed that with three more hits, including two doubles for a 4-4 afternoon. I was having the best April of my career. My hot month would continue the next night when the Chicago White Sox came to town. That night produced another 4-4 game. This time 2 singles, and 2 more doubles. After that game on the 27th I was hitting .512 for the month and had tied the Baltimore team record with eight consecutive hits. The streak would continue and eventually end the next night against Chicago. My 1st time up on the 28th I singled against Richard Dotson to give me nine straight hits: a new Oriole record. I was not quite finished. My next at bat I hit a rocket, but it was directly at White Sox second baseman Tony Bernazard who turned the hot grounder into a double play. I would end with a 2-4 night. After that game, I was hitting .511 as we closed in on the end of the month. The ten for ten streaks started and would end with a home run; in between four doubles and four singles.

-KEN SINGLETON

Right Field/DH, New York Mets, Montreal Expos, Baltimore Orioles, 3X All-Star, 1983 World Series Champion (Orioles)

I have had two Best Days:

1) Winning the 1st World Series in Philadelphia History
2) Watching the Cubs as General Manager in 1984 win their first Championship in 40 years.

-DALLAS GREEN

Pitcher; Philadelphia Phillies, Washington Senators, New York Mets, General Manager, Philadelphia Phillies, Chicago Cubs, New York Yankees, New York Mets, 1980 World Series Champion (Phillies), Phillies wall of fame

Best Day was opening day of the 2002 season, Expos vs Marlins. When the anthem was playing, I realized my dream had come true and a tear came down my face.

-MANNY ACTA

Third Base Coach; Montreal Expos, New York Mets, Seattle Mariners, Manager; Washington Nationals, Cleveland Indians

I have had many Best Days in Baseball, but two stand out for me. My 1st hit in the Big Leagues was a home run off Gary Peters, May 6, 1965 in Chicago when I was 20 years old. I guess my number one is winning the World Series in 1989 after the earthquake.

-RENE LACHEMANN

Catcher, Kansas City Athletics; Manager Seattle Mariners, Atlanta Braves, Chicago Cubs, Manager; Seattle Mariners, Milwaukee Brewers, Florida Marlins, Chicago Cubs

Best Day in Baseball:

Beating the Reds in 1973 League Championship Series- Game 2

-JON MATLACK

Pitcher, New York Mets, 3X All-Star, 1972 NL Rookie of the Year, 1973 NL Champions, 1973 Mets vs. Oakland A's World Series

Winning the Pennant in 1967

-KEN "The Hawk" HARRELSON
First Base / Outfield, Kansas City Athletics, Washington Senators, Boston Red Sox, Cleveland Indians,1968 All-Star, 1968 AL RBI Leader, Broadcast Announcer; Chicago White Sox

It was late August 1977, and a Sunday Game at Dodger Stadium against the Cardinals. I had been struggling…I hit two home runs; one was a grand slam, I had 5 RBI's, 5 hits, and 3 doubles.

-STEVE GARVEY

First Baseman, Los Angeles Dodgers, San Diego Padres; 10X All-Star, 1981 World Series Champion (Dodgers) and MVP, 4X Golden Glove Award

My Best Day as a pro player was winning the World Series in 1970 and being given the honor of being placed in the Orioles Hall of Fame.

-DON BUFORD

Left Field / 2nd Baseman / 3rd Baseman; Chicago White Sox, Baltimore Orioles, 1971 All-Star, 1970 MLB World Series Champion (Orioles)

My Best Day was my first game in the majors: first at bat; the swing and crack of the bat was the best feeling in the world.

-MAURY WILLS
Shortstop, Los Angeles Dodgers, Pittsburg Pirates, Montreal Expos, Manager; Seattle Mariners, 7X All-Star, 3X World Series Champion (Dodgers), 2X Golden Glove

My Best Day has not come yet!

-PETER UBERROTH
Commissioner of Baseball 1984-1989

I have had so many days that I can talk about playing in the Negro League against so many great Ball Players.

My all-time memory was when I played against Satchel Paige, June 1951 during the day in New Orleans.

Before the game I went down the right field line to warm up before the game. I must have thrown 100 pitches at least when I saw Satchel Paige going down the left field line to warm up. I threw pitch 101 and decided I was going to meet him. I walked around center field to left field. When I got 30 feet from him, he looked at me and I froze. I didn't know what to do. He said "you want to talk to me, boy? come over here and talk to me. You are pitching against me today?". I told him, "Yes, Sir." He asked how many innings I wanted to pitch? (I thought, are you kidding?) I told him nine innings, and he said you just pitched 5 innings over in right field show boating for the fans. He said. "We're going to light your little behind up in about the 4th inning, Boy." He said don't throw so many pitches warming up before a game. He said just throw about 15-18 pitches then put your jacket on and sit -down; and save your best for the game: he beat us 4 – 2.

Four weeks later I pitched against him again in Arkansas. I pitched 9 innings, WON 3-1! Satchel pitched 4 innings and gave up 2 runs.

He was the greatest Ball Player I ever met! The Greatest!

-JOHNNY WASHINGTON
Pitcher, New York Black Yankees, Baltimore Elite Giants

As to my Best Day in Baseball" I will offer two Best Days:

#1 My first Major League at bat with the St. Louis Cardinals & hitting a long home run.

#2 When my team, the Los Angeles Dodgers, won their first World Series by beating the Chicago White Sox in the fall of 1959.

-WALLY MOON

Outfield, St. Louis Cardinals, LA Dodgers, 3X All-Star, 3X World Series Champion (Dodgers)

Truly, my Best DF] 7ay in baseball has been a recurring theme. I've spent my entire life around the game, including every day of my adult life. I'm fortunate enough to have played at the highest level, as well as to build a post-playing career in a Major League front office. There have been so many highlights through the years, including, but limited to, what I would call my firsts. My first day as a professional player in 1989, first ML game in 1993 (among a lot of other ML first in 1993) the first trade I was connected with as a scout/executive in 2003, first draft I oversaw in 2009, first trade I made as interim GM in 2010 and here lately my moments along the way for me personally, as well as historic moments and milestone achievements I was fortunate enough to witness.

I have been blessed to spend my entire working life without ever feeling like I've worked a day. I've been fortunate enough to be exposed to and get to know childhood heroes that most people are never lucky enough to meet. Finally, I've had the opportunity to give back to the game itself and the fans who love it, which has been both a learning and consistently gratifying experience.

In the end, my answer to the question is that it would be impossible to site just one day in what has been a lifetime of great days!

JERRY DIPOTO
Pitcher, Cleveland Indians, NY Mets, Colorado Rockies, General Manager; Arizona Diamondbacks, CA Angels, Seattle Mariners

Best Day:

Perfect game against Senators at Shea Stadium for 7 2/3 innings. I finished with a 2 hitter; I don't remember the date. Greg Goosen and Dan Borsch got the hits.

-LARRY JASTER
Pitcher, Cardinals, Braves, Expos. 1967 World Series Champion (Cardinals)

Winning the 2003 World Series

JUAN PIERRE
Center Field / Left Field; Colorado Rockies, Florida Marlins, Chicago Cubs, Los Angeles Dodgers. Chicago White Sox; 2003 World Series Champion (Marlins), 3X Stolen Base Leader

Betty has passed away, but I know that Betty would have told the story that was written in the book "Dirt in the Skirt." Betty hit the winning run in the world series championship game.

-BETTY TREZZA

Utility, Minnesota Millerettes, Ft. Wayne Daisies, South Bend Blue Sox, Racine Belles; League Titles 1946, 1948

As far as my "Best Day" is concerned there have been so many "Best Days" in my personal life I can't not really pick out the number one Best Day.

But my Best Day in Sports was on October 22, 1980. It was the day following the final game of the sixth game of the 1980 World Series with the Philadelphia Phillies won to bring to Philadelphia their one and only World Championship in their 124-year history.

The City of Philadelphia produced a parade for the entire Philly organization and staff-all of whom were on floats with a few bands in the parade.

We travelled about six miles from the Philadelphia Museum of Arts to the old JFK Stadium. There were more than 2 million people along the parade route; and to observe their faces, smiles and adulation was so special it brought tears of joy to my eyes and heart.

People were hanging from light posts and everyone was dressed in Philly red- it was very, very, very special.

-BILL GILES
Co-Founder Houston Astros, Part Owner Philadelphia Phillies, Honorary President of National League 1934

I have had many personal accomplishments in my career that were noteworthy but recently I really enjoyed a "Best Day."

My wife and I returned to Dallas-Ft. Worth from a nine-day cruise on the Mediterranean to Italy. We flew home non-stop (12 hours) from Malta and arrived at 7:00 am DFW. It just happened that our troops arrived on a spate flight at the same time coming from Iraq. Passengers from both flights proceeded together through the terminal and near the baggage claim area, came upon hundreds and hundreds who had come from local churches to welcome home the troops. What a great feeling of patriotism to see, those men honored as they filed past the well-wishers. In this day and time of almost everything anti-this and anti that, it was a "Best Day" for me.

-CLAUDE OSTEEN
Pitcher, Cincinnati Redlegs, Washington Senators, Los Angeles Dodgers, Houston Astros, 3X All-Star, 1965 World Series Champion (Dodgers)

I hit two homers in the first inning, a total of 4 in the game; which tied a record, and we beat the White Sox 15-4.I am going to cherish this forever, I enjoyed the day to the utmost. This is the Best Day of my baseball career.

-MIKE CAMERON

Center Field, Chicago White Sox, Seattle Mariners, Cincinnati Reds, NY Mets, San Diego Padres, 2001 All-Star, 3X Golden Glove

I guess my Best Day was getting called up to the Big Leagues in May of 1975, after spending so much time in the minor leagues. Tough call to make.

-TOM KELLY

First Base, Minnesota Twins; Manager, Minnesota Twins, 2X World Series Champion (Twins), 1991 AL Manager of the Year

The birth of my son Charlie Rice Minoso.

-MINNIE MINOSO

Left Field, Cleveland Indians, Chicago White Sox, St Louis Cardinals, 9X All-Star, 3X Golden Glove, National Baseball Hall of Fame

I am sure your experience with health problems have given you, Mark, many thoughts and insight about Best Days.

Today is May 12, 2000 it's my Best Day so far.

-BOBBY KNOOP

2nd Baseman, Anaheim Angels, Chicago White Sox, Kansas City Royals, 1966 All-Star, 3X Golden Glove

The day I married my wife, Bette.

-RALPH HOUK
Catcher, New York Yankees, Manager; NY Yankees, Detroit Tigers, Boston Red Sox, 6X World Series Champion (Yankees, 3 each as a player & manager)

There is no question that the Best Day in my professional life was October 26th, 1997 when the Florida Marlins won the World Championship. This is the ultimate achievement for anyone associated with the game. Winning the Championship brought such great satisfaction to me and everyone else associated with the Marlin organization.

-DAVID DOMBROWSKI

President, Florida Marlins, Boston Red Sox, Detroit Tigers, Montreal Expos, 2X World Series Champion (Marlins & Red Sox), 3X AL Champion

The day I walked into the Yankee Clubhouse and met Whitey
Ford, Bobby Richardson, Yogi Berra, Mickey Mantle, & Roger
Maris as teammates!

-HAL STOWE
Pitcher, New York Yankees

Daddy always said if what you did yesterday is still important today, you haven't done enough today!

-CLYDE KING as told by Family of Clyde King
Pitcher, New York Yankees

Every day of my life is my Best Day.

-AL GRAMMAS

*Infielder, Saint Lewis Cardinals, Cincinnati Red Legs, Chicago Cubs,
Manager: Pittsburg Pirates, Milwaukee Brewers, Detroit Tigers, 2X World
Series Champion (Brewers & Tigers)*

It's hard to pinpoint a single day as "My Best Day" in baseball. After thinking about it I have come up with two instances I will mention.

The exhibition game against the Red Sox in San Diego and it was the final cut before the 1961 season. When I wasn't cut, I knew I was on my way to the Big Leagues!

The Chicago Cubs were playing the pennant winning Cincinnati Reds in late June or early July 1961. I was pitching the second game of a double header. We won the game 7-2 and I only threw 81 pitches in the nine-inning game. This brought my record to 4-2.

-JACK CARTER
Pitcher, Chicago Cubs, Milwaukee Braves, Cleveland Indians

My greatest day was in August 1951 when I got called up to the majors. I was playing in Dayton, OH class "A" ball when the manager Jim Crandall said he wanted a word with me.

That's when he said you are being called up to St Louis, the parent club. This was a dream come true. This was my goal since I was 9 years old. That's my story!

-JOHN "Bud" THOMAS
Short Stop, St Louis Browns

1st day in the Major Leagues. playing the Chicago White Sox 1962. I hit a homerun and we won the game 1-0. I also threw a guy out at 3rd.

-DON LOCK
Center Fielder, Washington Senators, Philadelphia Phillies, Boston Red Sox

Returning to the majors after doctors said I would never pitch again, Thanks to Kenny Myers, Dodger Scout, and my determination,

-ED ROEBUCK

Pitcher, Brooklyn/LA Dodgers, Washington Senators, 1955 World Series Champion (Dodgers)

My Best Day was a Sunday afternoon July 11, 1979 vs the New York Yankees. I went 5 for 5, with 2 doubles, 5 RBI's and with a 2-2 count in the bottom of the 9th, I hit a 2-run homerun to right center off Ron Guidry to win the game 5-4.

-BOBBY GRICH

Second Baseman, Baltimore Orioles, Anaheim Angels, 6X All-Star, 4X Golden Globe

My Best Day was when I won the Cy Young Award for the best pitcher in the league.

-JIM PERRY

Pitcher, Cleveland Indians, Minnesota Twins, Detroit Tigers, Oakland A's, 3X All-Star, 1970 AL Cy Young Award

When I was married to my wife who is the love of my life, and then the birth of my 3 children. I've been truly blessed. On a baseball note, when I made the New York Mets opening roster in 1984.

-JOHN GIBBONS
Catcher, New York Mets, Manager Toronto Blue Jays

Actually, I have had (4) "Best Days"-the birth dates of my four children.

-DAL MAXVILL

Short Stop/ 2nd Base; St Louis Cardinals, Oakland A's, Pittsburgh Pirates, 4X World Series Champion (3x Cardinals & 1x Pirates)

Some years ago, the late Michael Todd Jr. organized baseball games on a nice field down in Dobbs Ferry, NY. I was young then and could play a little shortstop, and one day I was beside Dick Tettelbach, who had played third base in the American League.

Stan Arblito, then athletic director at Columbia, cracked a line drive towards left center field. I went up as high as I could; the ball crashed into my glove and spun me in the air. I was a little stunned after I hit the ground, but not so stunned that I missed Dick Tettelbach," Major League play" I cannot think of a happier moment for me in sports.

-ROGER KAHN
Writer, "The Boys of Summer"

Friday, July 13th, 1973 I got called up to the Big Leagues.

-BILL CAMPBELL

Pitcher, Philadelphia Phillies, Minnesota Twins, Boston Red Sox, St. Louis Cardinals, All-Star

My Best Day will always be the 1st game of the 1959 World Series in Chicago. I went out into the dugout and just started out onto the field in a daze. This started out when I was 10 years old, always a dream to play in a World Series. So here it was 15 years later and what a beautiful dream came true.

-JIM LANDIS

Center Field, Chicago White Sox, Cleveland Indians, Houston Astros, Detroit Tigers, 2X All-Star, 5X Golden Glove

In 1951 I was pitching for the Hartford Chief (Class "A" Eastern League). I was given a night-going for my 20th win in Hartford against the Wilks Berma Team. I had been married 5 months before and they stopped the game and had my wife and I to receive some gifts in front of a full house of fans. It was the 7th inning, and the score was 0-0 and we finally won 2-0 and the catcher, Stanley Glenn, ran out and hugged me and said I reminded him of old Satch. I was named Minor League player of the year in 1953.

-GENE CONLEY

Pitcher, Milwaukee Braves, 2X All-Star, Center / Forward NBA; Boston Celtics, New York Knicks

The Best Day of my life was the day I was born.

-SAMMY SOSA

Right Field, Texas Ranger, Chicago Cubs, Baltimore Orioles, 7X All-Star, NL MVP, 6X Sliver Slugger Award

Mark, I was very fortunate to be able to play Major League Baseball for the many years that I did. It is hard for me to single out a day as it all was a childhood dream come true. But, as I reflect, my greatest thrill came at my first at bat in the 1979 World Series and hitting a two-run home run in my first at bat that ended up being the winning runs of that game. I had games in my career that I hit three HR's or walk off HR's or 4 for 4 days, but nothing can change the feeling I had running around the bases after the World Series HR. As I got to second base, my mind went back to all those days as a kid imitating stepping up to plate in a World Series (except I was playing with my friends in either over the line or wiffle ball). I do not even remember touching third base. Was so proud to have done it with my friends and family there to share it with as I became the 15th player in history to hit a HR in their first time at bat.

-DOUG DECINCES

Third Base, Baltimore Orioles, California Angels, St. Louis Cardinals, 1983 All-Star, 1982 Silver Slugger Award

I had several good moments while playing baseball. I pitched 3 no-hitters in pro ball. I pitched and batted in the winning run in the 19th inning of an All-Star Game.

-PAT MCGLOTHIN

Pitcher, Brooklyn Dodgers

In late August in 1957 I was playing in the outfield with the Hollywood Stars in the old PCL. I was hitting around .280 with 18 homeruns and 89 RBIs. I had set my goals during the season to hit at least .280 with 20 HR & 100 RBIs.

The last week of the season we went to Seattle and Portland. One night in Seattle I had one of the greatest nights of all time: I went 4-5, 2 HRs and 10 RBIs. I ended the season batting .284, 20 HRs and 102 RBIs! That night gave me a career day and enabled me to reach my goals for the year.

Pretty hard to top that!

-PAUL PETTIT
Pitcher/Outfielder, Pittsburgh Pirates

My Best Day I ever had was my no-hitter August 1, 1962 against the Chicago White Sox in Chicago against Hall of Famer Early Wynn.

-BILL MONBOUQUETTE
Pitcher, Boston Red Sox, Detroit Tigers, New York Yankees, San Francisco Giants, 4X All-Star, No Hitter August 1, 1962, Boston Red Sox Hall of Fame

Winning the World Series 1968.

My best game ever was July 1973 when I was the sixth person in Major League Baseball to hit two Grand Slams in one game.

-JIM NORTHRUP

Outfield, Detroit Tigers, Montreal Expos, Baltimore Orioles, 1968 World Series Champion (Tigers)

My Best Day was June 30, 1952 which was a month before my 20th birthday. I was lucky to brought up to the Red Sox in the middle of June 1952 and made two relief appearances and then got a start in Detroit and won 10-3. Then my next start was June 30, 1952 against the Yankees and across the river from my hometown of Boyonne, New Jersey. To put it in a nutshell we won 4-3 and I gave up 4 hits, 4 walks and had 8 strikeouts and a complete game.

-DICK BRODOWSKI
Pitcher, Boston Red Sox, Washington Senators, Cleveland Indians

My third win in the Major Leagues, I pitched against the Tigers and won.

-LOU LUCIER
Pitcher, Boston Red Sox, Philadelphia Phillies

Two Best Days:

1979-Winning American League West Championship and see the face of our owner, Gene Autry, and all the Angel Family that had never won a division championship before!

1993- Going to the World Series by beating the Atlanta Braves

-JIM FREGOSI

Shortstop, LA Angels, New York Mets, Texas Rangers, Pittsburg Pirates, Manager, CA Angels, Chicago White Sox, Philadelphia Phillies, Toronto Blue Jays, 6X All Star, 1967 Golden Glove Award, Angels Hall of Fame

My Major League debut; no hitter for 5 innings, May 15th, 1976.

-PETE REDFERN
Pitcher, Minnesota Twins

My Two Best Days:

First- Having 3 players we signed being hired to manage Major League Team: Larry Bowa (Phillies), Bob Boone (Reds) and Buck Martinez (Royals)

Second- in 1980 Phillies vs Kansas City in World Series, we signed (personally) 7 players that participated in the series: Bowa, Boone, Ruthven, Bob Walk, John Vukovich, Randy Lerch, Warren Brusstar- I am very proud of each one.

-EDDIE BOCKMAN
Third Base, New York Yankees, Cleveland Indians, Pittsburg Pirates

My best professional day(s) were two.

My first one came on September 17, 1983 when the Chicago White Sox clinched the American League West title with a victory over the Seattle Mariners. I will never forget the excitement of the fans in the Comiskey Park stands that night and the happiness everyone in the champagne-soaked clubhouse shared as they congratulated one another on the championship. My partner, Eddie Einhorn and I purchased the White Sox in 1981 and the 1983 division title was the first championship won by any Chicago sports team since the 1963 Chicago Bears. Despite winning two more division titles with the White Sox and six NBA World Championships with the Chicago Bulls, the first taste of winning in 1983 still rates as my Best Day.

My 2nd one was October 28, 2005. That was the day of the celebratory parade in Chicago after the White Sox won the 2005 World Series. Almost two million people lined the parade routes without a single bad incident. The happiness and love that showed in their eyes made me realize more than ever before what a baseball team means to a community.

-JERRY REINDORF
Owner, Chicago White Sox and Chicago Bulls

I had three personal marks of achievement laid out before me:

1) To be starting pitcher for the season opener
2) To be chosen for the All-Star Game
3) To pitch in the 1960 World Series

Another Best Day I remember was pitching both ends of a double header and getting the win for both games

-JIM COATES

Pitcher, New York Yankees, Washington Senators, Cincinnati Reds, LA/CA Angels, 2X All-Star, 2X World Series Champion (Yankees)

My best day in baseball was the day I hit three home runs against the New York Yankees in 1948. In 1948 the Indians won the World Series against the Boston Braves.

Two home runs in the first game of a double header, the second home run won the game.

Second game my home run tied the game, and we went on to win.

-EDDIE ROBINSON

First Baseman, Cleveland Indians, Washington Senators, Chicago White Sox, New York Yankees, 4X All-Star, 1948 World Series Champion (Indians)

Even though my career was over, my Best Day was when I was finally told that I couldn't get another operation to fix my shoulder after successfully getting the Tommy John surgery on my elbow. In a way, it was a release of pressure. I always went into every game trying to eliminate mistakes and survive yet another outing without disappointing my team and my teammates with a bad performance. I am very proud of my statistics and my career because I never allowed a bad outing to ruin a whole month or particularly a whole season.

On that day I sighed a breath of relief as I recalled I won more than I lost, managed to have a pretty good strike out to walk ratio, and ended up with an overall ERA that I'm very proud of: 2.75. That is more or less proof to me that I didn't let an extended period of failures happen.

-BOB LOCKER

Pitcher, Chicago White Sox, Milwaukee Brewers, Oakland A's, Chicago Cubs

Meeting my wife, Karen, because she saved my life. I had cancer, and at 90 years old, I am still here because of her.

As for a baseball Best Day, every day at the ballpark.

-DON NEWCOMBE

Pitcher, Brooklyn / Los Angeles Dodgers, Cincinnati Redlegs, Cleveland Indians, 4XAll- Star, NL MVP, Cy Young Award 1956, 1955 World Series Champion (Dodgers)

When I have been asked for my favorite memory, I have always stated that it was the day in August 1951, when I put on a Negro League uniform for the first time. To top it off, manager Marty Marion used me in relief that afternoon and I saved the game for Harry Brecken. Definitely a thrill!

-RICHARD BOKELMANN
Pitcher, St. Louis Cardinals

My Best Bay in baseball was my first day in the Majors. I went 3 for 5, hitting a triple and two singles.

-BOB TALBOT
Outfield, Chicago Cubs

In 1981 I led the Appalachian League in earned run average until I injured my shoulder late in the season. The St. Louis Cardinals released me and the Oakland A's signed me as a minor league free agent. Each day during Spring Training in 1982, we arrived at the practice fields at Arizona State where various rosters told us our assignments that day. It was a Saturday and I knew it was my day to pitch, but I could not find my name on the rosters of the Class A Modesto or Madison clubs; not the Double-A Huntsville or Triple-A Tacoma rosters. I began thinking this might be the A's way to tell me I was released, but my friend Dennis Gonsalves suggested I look at current list of players on the Oakland A's Major League roster. "Why?" I replied. "There's no way I've been called up to the big club."

But I looked at the roster and to my utter amazement, there I was: pitching innings four through six against the San Francisco Giants at Phoenix Municipal Stadium. I was pitching in a big-league exhibition game. The "show"!

I found a pay phone and called my dad, telling him to listen to the game, which would be broadcast back to California on both the Giants and A's networks. I had a car and drove to Phoenix Municipal Stadium. I arrived early. There were a handful of players getting in some work, taking grounders or hitting in the batting cages. A couple of coaches were working with them, but an astonishing sight met me.

Sitting on top of the home dugout in the lotus position was a gorgeous brunette in an eenie-weenie, teensie yellow bikini. She was lathered in suntan oil glistening on her tanned skin under the hot Arizona sun. I was like Slim Pickens in *Blazing Saddles*: "What in the wide, wide world of sports is goin' on here?"

One of the A's coaches was chatting her up. I was close enough to hear them talk. She was the wife of one of the A's other coaches and was "trolling for a date." When the coach asked about her husband she said, "He does what he wants, and I do what I want."

Whhhaaat!?

Of course, I had to focus on the job at hand, and eventually the girl left and the rest of the A's strolled out of the clubhouse. I do not remember anybody speaking to me. Most stared at me like, "Who's this guy?" or "What's this guy doing here?"

The game started, and only then did manager Billy Martin and his drinking buddy/pitching coach, Art Fowler, enter the dugout where both slumped in discomfort in the corner, like it was dive bar or something. They said little or nothing and did not seem to care about much. The previous evening had been a Friday in happening Scottsdale and I figured they had left their "A game" in a . . . dive bar. Finally, I made my way to the bullpen where former A's pitcher Dave Heaverlo, now a coach, was the only guy to encourage me. I warmed up and entered the game in the bottom of the fourth inning.

Now, this was just a Spring Training exhibition game, but it is important to note a few facts. First, it was a sellout crowd, perhaps 5,000 or 6.000 people. I was introduced by the P.A.

announcer to light applause, but my dad told me later that A's announcer Bill King seemed to know all about me. He called me a "lanky, 6-6 right-hander," and recalled the "glory days" of my high school career, and the fact I had been signed after pitching in the Cardinal chain. What a pro King was; he had taken the time to research a low-level minor league signee.

In fact, there were at least two Hall of Fame announcers in the booth that day. Lon Simmons, a Hall of Famer, was on the A's broadcast team with King, who will be inducted in the summer of 2017. I'm not sure if Lindsey Nelson or Hank Greenwald announced for San Francisco, but both those guys were legends.

Then there were the Hall of Famers playing in the game. Rickey Henderson was playing left field behind me. I pitched against Joe Morgan of the Giants. Both are in Cooperstown. There were other notable players in this game; Joe Rudi, Mickey Tettleton, and others. Hall of Famer Frank Robinson managed the Giants. Are you kidding me? As for me, well, I struck out seven batters in pitching three scoreless innings. I struck out Rob Deer two times. After the game, I was told I was starting the season at Modesto of the California League. Go to Baseball-Reference.com and check out the 1982 Modesto A's, one of the best minor league teams of all times. I did not make the Major Leagues and eventually was released, but I had my moments. That day at Phoenix Muni was my Best Day in the pros!

-STEVEN TRAVERS
Pitcher, Oakland A's, St Louis Cardinals

1986 World Series Championship

-DAVEY JOHNSON

Second base; Baltimore Orioles, Atlanta Braves, Philadelphia Phillies, Chicago Cubs, Manger; New York Mets, Cincinnati Reds, Baltimore Orioles, Los Angeles Dodgers, Washington Nationals, 4X All Star, 3X Golden Glover, 2X Manager of the Year, 3X World Series Champion (2x as a player Orioles & Mets as Manager)

My Best Day was May 24th, 1954 when the Pittsburg Pirates knocked the Brooklyn Dodgers out of first place in the NL Standings. I went 4-5 with one RBI and had a great game on defense.

-DICK COLE

Infielder, St. Louis Cardinals, Pittsburg Pirates, Milwaukee Braves

The first time up and we were playing the Detroit Tigers. Hal Newhouse was pitching and my first time up, I hit a three bagger and was so happy.

-LEN OKRIE
Catcher, Washington Senators, Boston Red Sox

One of my Best Days was when I was 16 year's old, and I had joined the ball club for the 1943 season. For quite a while I was just pitching batting practice; and then I was asked to make a road trip with the club. On the way back to Philadelphia, Connie Mack called me to come into his room. Few words were spoken, he said to me don't you think it's about time. And I replied, I'm ready. Reaching Philadelphia, my father had to come, and we signed a contract, and that day & that time I pitched in my first game.

Another Best Day, 43 and 44 seasons I just mopped up games. 45-46 I was in the service. I came back for the 1947 season, and for a short while I was mopping up games again. Finally, I got my chance to start a game in Detroit and I won it 4-0. That was one of my Best Days, "What a feeling"

Another "Best Day" was when I hit a bases loaded home run. Pitchers were not known to be hitters.

Another "Best Day" was a walk-on pinch hitter, got a hit to win the game.

-CARL SCHEIB
Pitcher, Philadelphia A's, St. Louis Cardinals

104

The two days that I beat the Yankees were the highlight of my baseball career. Not only did I have one Best Day, but another week later I had another one. It was my American League debut and we won 7-6 in ten innings in the first game; and we won 5-4 a week later; plus, I hit the game winning home run.

-STEVE NAGY
Pitcher, Pittsburgh Pirates, Washington Senators

1973 as Manager of the Kansas City Royals, my hometown of South Amboy, NJ gave me a day at Yankee Stadium in New York. During the ceremonies with my family (wife, children, mother, sister-brother) all present, my mother whispered in my ear, "Boy would your dad be proud of you today" I had tears in my eyes with that remark.

My dad was my biggest booster and he died in 1966. I only wish he could have been there, but I know he was in there in spirit.

-JACK MC KEON
Manager, KC Royals, Oakland A's, San Diego Padres, Cincinnati Reds, Florida Marlins, 2X NL Manager of the Year, San Diego Padres Hall of Fame, 2003 World Series Champion (Marlins)

My Best Day was having to play and coach in the Big Leagues.
There was nothing like it.

-ROCKY BRIDGES

*Center Field / Third Base, Brooklyn Dodgers, Cincinnati Reds, Washington
Senators, Detroit Tigers, 1958 All-Star*

My Best Day was in Seattle while playing for the White Sox in 1977. I hit for the cycle. 1st two at bats were doubles, then a home run, followed by a single. My last at bat our Manager Bob Lemon told me if I get a hit to not stop until I reach third. I hit a gapper and made it to third.

-JACK BROHAMER
Second Base, Cleveland Indians, Chicago White Sox, Boston Red Sox

My Best Day in baseball: I caught Nolan Ryan's 2nd no hitter on July 15, 1973 in Detroit. He struck out 17 hitters, which is the most in a no hitter.

-ART KUSNYER

Catcher, Chicago White Sox, California Angels, Milwaukee Brewers, Kansas City Royals

Sorry you have had such bad luck- thanks for being a Yankee fan.

My Best Day is every day I wake up feeling food and in good health- I thank God for that.

-BOBBY MURCER

Right Field / Left Field, New York Yankees, SF Giants, Chicago Cubs, 5X All-Star, Golden Glove Award

My first Best Day was when I pitched a 14-inning complete game against the tough New York Yankees in Yankee Stadium and beat them 2-1. I believe it was June 6, 1952.

Having grown up being a Cardinal fan and a Stan Musial fan, my most memorable day came on the last day of the season in 1963. We played the Cubs, and it was Musial's last game. At the conclusion of the game he and his wife were driven around the stadium in a convertible. Upon arriving at home plate, I saw tears streaming down his face. There were not many dry eyes in the stands either.

I realized how lucky I was to have played with my hero, and to have seen the last game of his Hall of Fame Career.

-BOBBY SCHANTZ
Pitcher, Philadelphia/KC Athletics, New York Yankees, Pittsburg Pirates, St, Louis Cardinals, 3X All-Star, 8X Golden Glove, 1958 World Series Champion (Yankees)

It is difficult to pick a "My Best Day in Baseball" as I had been very blessed over my whole career. The day I was drafted the #1 overall pick in the 1974 draft was a huge day for me. It set the tone for the rest of my career as I would always be the #1 pick. Playing in my first MLB game for the Padres against the Braves on September 2, 1974 was another Best Day as not only did I fulfill my dream of playing the Big Leagues, but I also got my first MLB hit. I also remember when I was with the Pirates in 1986 having a game winning, walk off extra inning inside the park home run against the Astros. There were a number of four hit days that were special too.

-BILL ALMON

Infielder, San Diego Padres, Montreal Expos, New York Mets, Chicago White Sox, Oakland Athletics

Arriving in the Major League which completed my goal I set for myself. Walking on the field and the game I loved.

-SAM EWING

Out Field/ Designated Hitter; Chicago White Sox, Toronto Blue Jays

Getting the call to the Major Leagues on June 15, 1977. First night in the Major Leagues Nolan Ryan was starting pitcher for Angels in Minnesota.

-RANCE MULLINIKS

*Third Base / Short Stop, California Angels, Kansas City Royals,
Toronto Blue Jays*

Every day I was playing was a Best Day

-HAL KELLER

Catcher; Washington Senators, Vice President of Operations Seattle Mariners

The day I was voted MVP of the 1972 World Series.

-GENE TENACE

*Catcher/ 1st Baseman; Oakland A's, San Diego Padres, St Louis Cardinals,
1975 All Star, 4X World Series Champion (3X A's & 1X Cardinals) Manager;
Toronto Blue Jays, 1993 World Series Champions (Toronto)*

My Best Day was my first game in the Major Leagues, first start in the Major Leagues I pitched 7 or 8 innings and won the game against Baltimore, 3 to 2.

I guess the best and worst day was in Cleveland. I lost a complete game 1-0. The loss was to Herb Score, it was the only game he won after getting hit in the eye by a line drive.

-TED WILLS

Pitcher; Boston Red Sox, Cincinnati Reds, Chicago White Sox

I think my Best Day was when I was playing AA ball and Montreal Royals called me to AAA ball. Since I was born Canadian, Montreal was the Big Leagues to me. In the 1950's our team in Montreal could have played in the Majors.

-BILL HARRIS

Pitcher, Brooklyn/ Los Angeles Dodgers, Canadian Baseball Hall of Fame

It was my one and only appearance in an All-Star Game in 1979. The location was my hometown ballpark, the Seattle Kingdome, which made it all the more special. Going to the locker room before the game and suiting up with all the best players in the American League was like a dream-Ryan, Guidry, Jackson, Yastrzemski, Rice, Lynn, Brett, etc. The game itself was a thriller. Back and forth the lead changed a number of times. I was put in as a pinch hit in the 6th inning with the game tied. I managed to get a base hit on an 0-2 count off Gaylord Perry to put the American League ahead. This gave us the momentary possibility of breaking the 7 or 8 year spell the National League held over the Americans in All Star competition. I got to the plate again in that game with a runner on first. Manager Bob Lemon directed me to bunt which I did successfully against Bruce Sutter. Reggie Jackson was on deck and they walked him so there was some question whether Lemon should have allowed me to hit. The National League came up with a couple of runs late in the game to garner the win. In spite of the loss it was a wonderful day and the most memorable of my career.

-BRUCE BOCHTE

Utility/ Left Field/ 1st Baseman; CA Angels, Cleveland Indians, Seattle Mariners, Oakland A's, 1979 All Star

My Best Day was in 1952. I came home late at night from work. When I walked in the door, my father said, hold it. I stopped and he told me the Pirates had called and said Mr. Rickey had drafted me from the Pacific Coast League, to play in the Big Leagues with the Pirates.

-ELROY FACE

Pitcher; Pittsburg Pirates, Detroit Tigers, Montreal Expos, 6X All Star, 1960 World Series Champion (Pirates)

My best day was my no-hitter on April 30, 1946 at Yankee Stadium.

-BOB FELLER

Pitcher, Cleveland Indians, 8X All Star, 1948 World Series Champion (Indians), Cleveland Indians Hall of Fame, National Baseball Hall of Fame

My Best Day was in the World Series: the Brooklyn Dodgers and the New York Yankees. It was at Yankee Stadium, 6th game, I was a bench player- infielder and catcher-and I did not bat in the first 5 games. I was in the bullpen to warm up pitchers, but in the 7th inning our manager, Burt Shelton (filling in for suspended Leo Durocher) called the bullpen and said have Bragan come up and hit for pitcher Ralph Branca. I had invited my mother and father to come to the Series from Florida, and they had watched the 1st five games without seeing me go to bat. So, when I got a two-base hit off Joe Page they were in the restrooms. But the thrill was present; and they enjoyed the Series. The Yankees won the next day, so we lost the series, 4 games to 3.

I'll never forget my Best Day.

-BOBBY BRAGAN

Catcher & Infielder; Brooklyn Dodgers, Manager- Pittsburg Pirates, Cleveland Indians, Milwaukee Brewers, Atlanta Braves

I have had many "Best Days" in my nearly 80 years of life. Playing a game, baseball, and having it take me all over the world; having my dream of reaching the Major Leagues come true; having a wonderful wife, 2 great kids and grandkids; and having good health.

But after reading the amazing chronology of what you have gone through and are still "ticking", I must admit that your will to keep going against all odds truly makes my "Best Day".

-GLENN MICKENS
Pitcher; Brooklyn Dodgers, Kintetsu Buffaloes

My Best Day in baseball started out as not so good of a day as I had been real sick the previous three day prior to my Best Day- April 17th, 1974. It was my fifth home game of my first year with the Cubs. My wife was out looking for a place for us to live in Chicago. We had two small children and were staying with some friends we met in Minnesota when I was with the Twins.

We were playing the Pittsburg Pirates that day. The first time up, the bases were loaded, and I hit a grand slam homerun, my first in the Big Leagues. The second time up there was a runner on and I hit another home run. Two at bats with 6 RBI's and 2 homeruns. The third time up, the bases were loaded again. This time I walked for another RBI. By the time my wife had heard on the radio I was having a day to remember. She got to the ballpark just after she got to see this one, The fifth time up a man was on first, and I hit one off the top of the left field wall for a double and the runner couldn't score as I had hit the ball harder than the three homeruns. All in all, it was a day everyone dreams of!

FINAL STATS:

Pittsburg 9   Chicago 18

3 HRS- 1 double-14 total bases; still a Cubs record and 8-10 standing ovations- 1 Happy Wife!

-GEORGE MITTERWALD
Catcher; Minnesota Twins, Chicago Cubs

124

My Best Day was 1974 actually lasted only a few minutes. In 1974 I was called up from my four years in Minor League Baseball to the Major Leagues with the Kansas City A's. After driving all night, I arrived in KC in the middle of their game with the Minnesota Twins. I got a uniform on and went to the bull pen. I just had time to shake hands with the other pitchers and the phone rang to tell me to warm-up "quickly". After the batter reached base, I was moved in. Bases were loaded, tie game, 7th inning, and Bob Allison was the batter. On my first Major League pitch he hit a short fly ball to left field; runners did not advance. Next batter (I had heard of) was Harmon Killebrew. He hit my 2nd pitch to the short stop, and we got a double play. Feeling that the Major Leagues was not so tough I walked to the dugout. 1 inning, 0 hits, 0 runs, 3 pitches. My childhood dream had come true!

-JACK AKER

Pitcher, Kansas City / Oakland A's, New York Yankees, Chicago Cubs, Atlanta Braves, New York Mets

So far, the "Best Day" in my life would have to be in June 2001, when the Red Sox drafted me in the 8th round. All my hard work, dedication & lifelong dreams were finally coming true. I was accepted into professional baseball and given the opportunity to prove myself.

-KEVIN YOUKILIS

First & Third Baseman, Boston Red Sox, Chicago White Sox, New York Yankees, 3X All-Star, 2X World Series Champion (Red Sox), 2007 Golden Glover

Finding out my oldest son was going to live after a boating accident took his left leg.

-GEORGE VUKOVICH

Right Field, Philadelphia Phillies, Cleveland Indians, 1980 World Series Champion (Phillies)

I think the first "Best Day" would be when my lovely wife, Sharon, and I were married on September 28, 1976, over 33 years ago. In succeeding years, each time one of our 5 children were born could qualify as a "Best Day".

In 1986, a month following the birth of our 3rd child, our 2nd child, Natalie was diagnosed with a malignant brain tumor. Following surgery, chemotherapy, and radiation every 6 months she required a CAT scan check up to be sure the tumor had not returned. Every 6 months, the anxiety would rise as that day approached and each time for the next 5 years, I was blessed to have a "Best Day" as the results were negative. My wife and I would cry and hold each other as we read the results that were handed to us in a sealed envelope.

Now my Best Days are witnessing my children achieve or display their numerous talents whether in a ball game, a speech, service others as missionaries for our LDS church, or a piano recital. My oldest son and his wife have 2 beautiful children, our first grandchildren, and each time I can have a grandpa day with them is a "Best Day." All my Best Days, center around my family and the great times that we can spend together and constitute the blessed life that I have had.

My "Best Day' in baseball could be the day I got drafted in the 29th round that got my dream of playing professional baseball started. It could be the day I got called up to the Major Leagues for the Pittsburg Pirates and got my first hit off Tom Hausman of the Mets. It could be my first home run off Hall of Famer, Gaylord Perry. My "Best Day" could be the day I found out I was selected to the National League All Star team in 1988 and was one of 6 Cubs to be selected that year. It could be winning the AL West Division with the White Sox in 1983 and in the NL East Division with the Cubs in 1989. It might be one of the 2 home run games that I had or the walk off grand slam in the bottom of the 9th off the Pirates while I was with the Expos. It also could be the day I played catch in the Chicago Cubs clubhouse with President Ronald Regan prior to him throwing out the 1st pitch at Wrigley Field. He threw the 1st ball up on top of the lockers and I had to climb up and get it so we could continue. He did much better when he took the mound. It might be the days that I met Willie Mays, Joe DiMaggio, Bob Gibson, Billy Williams, or Ernie Banks.

Again. I was blessed to have so many great experiences that I cannot single one out. My 10 years in the Major Leagues career passed so quickly it seems now like it was only a day so in those terms, that was a "Best Day."

-VANCE LAW

3rd Baseman, Pittsburg Pirates, Chicago White Sox, Montreal Expos, Oakland A's, Chicago Cubs, 1988 All-Star

My Best Day, playing against my role model, Ernie Banks, who signed an autograph for me in 1960 when I was 12 years old & said to me, "I'll see you in the Big Leagues"

-DARRELL CHANEY
Shortstop, Cincinnati Reds, Atlanta Braves, 1975 World Series Champion (Reds)

Opening day, Anaheim 1966 -in attendance was Walt Disney, Ronald Reagan, and Hall of Famer Tommy John!

-RICK REICHARDT

Outfield, California Angels; Washington Senators, Chicago White Sox, Kansas City Royals

I've had a lot of Best Days. One of those days was when I was called to the Major Leagues for the first time. I was able to play in front of family and friends my entire career.

-FRANK WHITE

Second Baseman, Kansas City Royals, 5X All-Star, 1985 World Series Champion (Royals), 8X Golden Glove

My best moment in baseball had to be in 2004. It was my second year in the Big Leagues, and we had just opened a new stadium in San Diego. We were playing the Giants on opening night and I had a big part in the victory over the Giants. I went 3-4 that night, tied the game in the 8th with a two-out single and eventually won it in the bottom of the tenth for a 4-3 victory. What a great feeling.

-SEAN BURROUGHS

Third Base; San Diego Padres, Tampa Bay Devil Rays, Arizona Diamondbacks, Minnesota Twins

My Best Day in baseball was in 1975 when I scored the 1 millionth run at Candlestick Park- seconds ahead of Dave Concepcion. I scored on Milt Mays's homerun for the Astros- it's a record that will always be on the books for MLB. What a thrill!

Game 1 of the 1981 World Series: 1st at bat I hit a 3-run Home Run.

-BOB WATSON

First Base / Left Field, Houston Astros, Boston Red Sox, NY Yankees, Atlanta Braves, 2X All-Star, General Manager; Houston Astros, MLB VP Rules & On-Field Operations

My Best Day was reaching the goal of 400 career home runs in 1999. I was only the
28th Major League player to reach that level- it was a fantastic feeling.

-JOSE CANSECO

Outfielder / DH, Oakland A's; Texas Rangers, Boston Red Sox, Toronto Blue Jays, NY Yankees, Chicago White Sox, 6X All-Star, 2X World Series Champion (A's & Yankees), 4X Silver Slugger Award

The moment I hit the ball for a home run in the bottom of the 9th inning to win game 1 in the 1988 World Series was the absolute Best Day of my life in sports. I was hurt and could barely walk. If it was not a home run, I never could have outrun a base hit. That feeling is indescribable. I know it's a classic highlight- I did it for our team, Tommy Lasorda and the whole staff, the fans, and my family, the thrill and joy from that game will be in my heart always.

-KIRK GIBSON

Outfielder, Detroit Tigers, LA Dodgers, KC Royals, Pittsburg Pirates, Detroit Tigers, Manager Arizona Diamondbacks, 2X World Series Champion (Tigers / Dodgers), 1988 Silver Slugger Award

July 29th, 1978 was my Best Day-It was such a great moment. It was old timers' day at Yankee Stadium, it was announced that I was returning to manage the Yankees. Not only were players I managed there, but my old teammates on the field. I got a standing ovation. It was the greatest moment of my career.

-BILLY MARTIN

Second Baseman, NY Yankees, KC Royal, Detroit Tigers, Cleveland Indians, Cincinnati Reds, Manager, Minnesota Twins, Detroit Tigers, Texas Rangers, NY Yankees, Oakland A's, 1956 All-Star, 5X World Series Champion (4X Yankees as a player / 1X Yankees as a Manager)

I will be forever thankful for this Best Day, being elected into the Pro Baseball Hall of Fame. I toiled over the choice to represent the Angels over the Montreal Expos (Now Washington Nationals) for a long time, Canadian people mean a whole lot to me. Picking the Angels means a lot because of what it represents, with all the winnings.

My mom was with me when I received the news. There was joy all over the house. It is a beautiful moment.

-VLADIMIR GUERRERO
Right Field / DH, Montreal Expos, Anaheim Angels, Texas Rangers, Baltimore Orioles, 9X All-Star, 2004 AL MVP, 8X Silver Slugger, National Baseball Hall of Fame

Getting a new heart in 2016 saved my life was my Best Day so far. Former NFL player, Konrad Reuland, died of a brain aneurysm at the age of 29 and was an organ donor. The gift of time has so many meanings. Konrad and I are always together now, and we're going to do good things together by spreading the word about tissue and organ donation. The "Heart of 29" campaign; named for Konrad's age that he passes as well as my baseball number, has partnered with the American Heart Association to promote donations. Konrad has given me the greatest gift any person can give another.

-ROD CAREW
First Base / Second Base; Minnesota Twins, Anaheim Angels, 18X All-Star, 7X AL Batting Champion, National Baseball Hall of Fame

Signing as the Yankee's manager is the best, what a great day. What an honor- the Yankee Program is storied. I would say in a way I've been preparing for this job for the last 44 years.

-AARON BOONE

Third Baseman; Cincinnati Reds, NY Yankees, Cleveland Indians, Florida Marlins, Washington Nationals, 2003 All-Star; Manager; New York Yankees

Breaking Yogi Berra's record by hitting 307 home runs for the most HR's by a catcher was my Best Game as a player. I had 3 RBI's, and my White Sox beat the Yankee's 7-3 in 1989. Ironically, the Yankee's was Yogi's team.

-CARLTON FISK

Catcher, Boston Red Sox, Chicago White Sox, 11X All-Star, 1972 AL Rookie of the Year, National Baseball Hall of Fame

The craziest, Best Moment as a ball player for me was September 2nd, 1971 when I hit a fly ball in the 5th inning that was an inside-the-park grand slam after Jim Lefebvre and Bill Buckner of the Dodgers ran into each other. It was such a fluke, so unbelievable and an amazing feeling.

-CESAR CEDENO

Center Field, Houston Astros, Cincinnati Reds, St. Louis Cardinals, Los Angeles Dodgers, 4X All-Star, 5X Golden Glove

Winning the 1988 World Series was my greatest day ever! As a little boy I dreamed of pitching in the World Series and being on the cover of Sports Illustrated. I threw the final, winning pitch of the game and made the SI cover-both dreams that came true!

-OREL HERSCHISER

Pitcher, LA Dodgers, Cleveland Indians, SF Giants, NY Mets, 3X All-Star, 1988 World Series Champion & MVP (Dodgers), Golden Glove

Obviously, induction into the Hall of Fame is one of the greatest honors of my life. The best thing, my best day, though, that's ever happened to me is the day Andrea agreed to marry me. She is without a doubt the best teammate I could ever have.

Another baseball Best Day was hitting a home run at home for the Chicago White Sox at home with my family in attendance was special. But my Best Day I've ever spent in baseball was at the Baseball Hall of Fame when I delivered the ball that I hit my 500th homerun with. I had a great time spending time in the exhibit halls, and seeing an archive folder that had a picture of my father and brother playing in a semipro league, as well as a picture of my Aunt at her induction into the American Softball Association Hall of Fame.

-JIM THOME
First Baseman / DH / Third Baseman; Cleveland Indians, Philadelphia Phillies, Chicago White Sox, Los Angeles Dodgers, Minnesota Twins, Baltimore Orioles, 5X All-Star, 1996 Silver Slugger Award, 2003 NL Home Run Leader, National Baseball Hall of Fame

I have spent 12 seasons in the minors, and I got my first start today (7/27/17) my very first Major League hit was a three-run homer, amazing! A great moment, I have waited so long for this. After twelve years in the minor leagues, when they called me last night, it was the best day of my life. I cried.

-FRANCISCO ARCIA

Catcher, Anaheim Angels

I've had so many memorable game days in my career, but my best day as a Giant was August 1st, 1977. I hit two home runs that day, one was a grand slam that was my 18th career grand slam. It's still a National League record and a wonderful memory.

Second to that, having "McCovey Cove" outside the new Stadium named after me was cool.

-WILLIE MCCOVEY

First Baseman, SF Giants, San Diego Padres, Oakland A's, 6X All-Stars, 3X NL home run leader, National Baseball Hall of Fame

I looked on my phone and saw Billy Eppler, Angels Manager, was calling. I knew the call meant one thing; someone was getting a call up to the Majors. Little did I know it was going to be me! It's one of my best moments in my life, and certainly my best moment so far in baseball, I'll never forget.

-KEITH JOHNSON

Infielder; Angels, Manager; AAA Baby Cakes for Miami Marlins

Other than playing golf and the first day as a Major League Player...my first hit was my Best Day; Because you never know if it may be the only one you'll ever get by playing in the pros. Going to work with the same guys every day, and you never know if they will always be there, or if I would be there? I always ended the practice with a hit on base, I didn't want to end the day with a miss or a strike. Getting to the World Series, that was the height of my playing. For each hit, I look at two parts of the game. One, I would like a line drive to be hit so hard to an infielder that it hits his face, and two, if you are on 1st base and you get a juke step or something.

-DAVE WINFIELD

Right Field; San Diego Padres, NY Yankees, CA Angels, Toronto Blue Jays, Minnesota Twins, 12X All Star, 1992 World Series Champion (Blue Jays), 7X Golden Glove, 6X Silver Slugger, National Baseball Hall of Fame

Even before I got drafted, when I was a little kid, you want to play in the World Series. Now the Dodgers are going to the World Series, and it is my Best Day. It is all I have ever dreamed about.

-CLAYTON KERSHAW
Pitcher; Los Angeles Dodgers, 8X All Star, 2014 NL MVP, 3X Cy Young Winner

This day is the best, winning the Astro's first World Series (2017), it is the absolute best. It's a crazy journey, man. I was the only one on the team from 2011-2013 and those 100 losses…three years in a row. I always believed we were going to become good, and the heart of this team proved it.

-JOSE ALTUVE

Second Baseman; Houston Astros, 6X All Star, AL MVP 2017, 5X Silver Slugger, 3X AL batting champion, World Series Champion 2017 (Astros)

Winning the World Series (2017) was the best. As a kid it was a dream, while playing baseball in the backyard with my brother. I dreamt of this! Seeing the smiles on my teammates as they rushed the field, it is my Best Day, a great Best Day.

-ALEX BREGMAN

Third Baseman / Short Stop; Houston Astros, 2X All Star, 2017 World Series Champion (Astros)

I've had two personal Best Days in my baseball career. On this day, April 28, 1989 I broke a record that I was tied with Bobby Bonds on. I set the MLB record of 36 leadoff home runs. That record is special, along with my record of the most stolen bases. I broke Lou Brocks record on May 1st, 1991 with 939 stolen bases. Both of those milestones mean a lot to me.

-RICKY HENDERSON

Left Fielder; Oakland A's, NY Yankees, Toronto Blue Jays, San Diego Padres, Anaheim Angels, NY Mets, 10X All Star, 2X World Series Champion (A's) 3X Silver Slugger, 12X AL stolen base leader, Oakland A's Hall of Fame & retired number 24, National Baseball Hall of Fame

Wow, oh man! Pitching a no-hitter today (May 8, 2018) for the Mariners here in my native Canada is the perfect place for the best game and Best Day of my life. I cannot believe that I am the very first Canadian no-hitter in Canada. You couldn't write this stuff. Pretty amazing to have it happened against the Blue Jays, at home in Canada. The fans were great, they were cheering me on because I am Canadian, pretty cool.

-JAMES PAXTON
Pitcher; Seattle Mariners, New York Yankees

My best game ever was May 23, 2002 vs. Milwaukee, I was the 14th player ever to hit four homeruns in one game, and I set a MLB record with 19 total bases. I went 6 for 6, scored 6 runs with 7 RBI's. What a feeling, and it was my Best Day in Baseball.

-SHAWN GREEN

Right Field; Toronto Blue Jays, Los Angeles Dodgers, Arizona Diamondbacks, New York Mets, 2X All Star, 1999 Golden Glove and Silver Slugger

Being on the greatest team, the Pirates, during the "We Are Family" era was my Best Days as a player. It was an amazing group of guys and coaches, and we had the best fans. To cap it off with the World Series- just the Best Ever.

-WILLIE STARGELL

Left Fielder/ First Baseman; Pittsburg Pirates, 7X All Star, 2X World Series (Pirates), 1979 NL MVP & World Series MVP, 2X Homerun leader, Pittsburg Pirate # 8 retired, National Baseball Hall of Fame

I would say my Best Day and Best Day in baseball was in May 1976. I was the winning pitcher for Houston vs. the Braves. What made it so special was that I hit my only home run in my 22-year career, and it was off my brother, Phil Niekro.

-JOE NIEKRO

Pitcher; Chicago Cubs, San Diego Padres, Detroit Tigers, Atlanta Braves, Houston Astros, New York Yankees, Minnesota Twins, 1979 All Star, 1987 World Series Champion, Houston Astros Hall of Fame

My Best Day was and is every night when I go to bed, I'm very thankful that I had another day that I spent, or talked to, or even remembered about spending time with my family and friends, especially my grandchildren: Chase and Emma Catherine.

-PHIL NIEKRO

Pitcher; Milwaukee / Atlanta Braves, New York Yankees, Cleveland Indians, Atlanta Braves, 5X All-Star, 5X Golden Glover, 2X NL wins leader, No-hitter August 5, 1973, National Baseball Hall of Fame

Oh wow! Today is my greatest day. It's my first pro start and I am the youngest ballplayer in the Majors to hit a home run. We won the game, too. Today is a dream come true.

-JUAN SOTO

Outfielder; Washington Nationals, 2019 All-Star, 2019 World Series Champion (Nationals)

Best Days:

1) 1970- the day I was told that I made the All-Star team

2) 1965 – 18 years old, 2 at bats: 1st hit was a home run off Grant, I believe I am the youngest player to ever hit a pinch-hit home run.

-GERRY MOSES
Catcher; Boston Red Sox, CA Angels, Cleveland Indians, NY Yankees, Detroit Tigers, 1970 All Star

My Best Day(s), excluding marrying Suree French and the birth of our three children and ten grandchildren:

1) Graduating from the Tulane University School of Medicine, June 6,1950.

2) Hitting a pinch hit double in game seven of the 1947 World Series Game, Yankees vs Brooklyn Dodgers. The double drove in the tying run and put the go ahead run on third. Yankees won the game, (5-2) and the Series. I had a pinched hit three times prior to game seven, a base on balls, a double, and a single.

-BOBBY BROWN

Third Baseman, New York Yankees, 4X World Series Champion (Yankees), Elected Sixth President of the American League

Easter Sunday 1987, Brewers vs. Rangers

The Brewers trail 4-1 in the bottom of the 9th. Rob Deer hit a 3-run homerun to tie the game. Dale Sveum hit a 2-run homer to win the game. The Brewers record moved to 12-0. I started that game for Brewers and was proud to be a part of such a magical ending. I still get chills.

-MIKE BIRKBECK
Pitcher; Milwaukee Brewers, New York Mets

161

My best moment was pitching my first Big League game in a 9th inning relief job against the Chicago White Sox who led us (Detroit) by one run. I had the privilege of pitching against Nellie Fox and George Kell, two greats and managed to get them and Sandy Consuegra (pitcher) on an off day. We had runners on base in the bottom of the 9th, but the Sox won, and omen perhaps.

-JIM BRODY
Pitcher, Detroit Tigers

After reading your letter and incredible story, I would love to contribute to your book project.

On May 3, 2009 the Chicago Cubs retired my number 31 along with another great pitcher, Greg Maddux. I joined an elite group that included some of my teammates and close friends, Ernie Banks, Billy Williams, and Ron Santo. To me that moment was incredibly special since I was being honored by an organization that I loved and deeply respected. I bled cubby blue for 10 years (and one as a coach) and seeing all those fans cheering while I was on the field took me back to the many days spent there with Ernie, Billy, Glenn Beckert, and all the other great Cub players I played with. You go on the mound every fourth day and you do the best you can, I was lucky my best was usually good enough to keep us in the game and the fans really appreciate it.

Cub fans are the greatest in the world and 25 years after pitching on that mound for the last time it was magical to feel the energy from the crowd, to feel those electric shivers running up your spine knowing that 30,000 plus people are supporting you…you feed off of that.

-FERGUSON JENKINS

Pitcher; Philadelphia Phillies, Chicago Cubs, Texas Rangers, Boston Red Sox 3X All-Star, NL 1972 Cy Young Winner, Chicago Cubs retired #31, National Baseball Hall of Fame

Every day is a Best Day.

Winning a World Series was a Best Day, so was 4 Homeruns in one game.

Another Best Day was watching my Godson, Barry Bonds, play in the majors.

I have had too many to pick!

-WILLIE MAYS

Center Field; New York / San Francisco Giants, New York Mets, 24X All-Star, 1954 World Series Champion (SF Giants), 2X NL MVP, 12X Golden Glove Winner, 4X Home Run Leader, 4X Stolen Base Leader, April 30, 1961 hit 4 HR's in one game, San Francisco Giants #24 retired & Wall of Fame, MLB ALL-Century Team, MLB All-Time Team, National Baseball Hall of Fame

My Best Day happened, believe it or not, when I failed to hit my one and only home run in the Majors. On that day, I hit a single, double and triple and flied out to the left field warning track on my last at bat! I ended up going 3 for 4 RBI's with the Minnesota Twins in 1977.

-LUIS GOMEZ

Short Stop, Minnesota Twins, Toronto Blue Jays, Atlanta Braves

My Best Day was done in two days in 1952, May 15th and August 25th- the two no-hitters I pitched!

-VIRGIL "Fire" TRUCKS

Pitcher; Detroit Tigers, St. Louis Browns, Chicago White Sox, Kansas City Athletics, New York Yankees, 2X All-Star, World Series Champion (1x as a player Tigers / 1x as a Coach Yankees), Pitched 2 no-hitters, 1949 MLB strikeout leader, Coach; Pittsburg Pirates

Perhaps my "Best Offensive Day'- was when I went 3 for 4,3 RBI's, 2 of my hits were homeruns and I won the game against Cleveland with a bunt single. For someone with a lifetime batting average of .219 and 16 lifetime home runs, this game more than qualifies as a Best Day.

-BILLY HUNTER

Short Stop; St Louis Browns / Baltimore Orioles, New York Yankees, Kansas City Athletics, Cleveland Indians, 1953 All-Star, Baltimore Orioles Hall of Fame, Manager; Texas Rangers

My Best Day in baseball came during the playoffs in 2000. I was playing for the Giants and we were in New York. My son Jason was allowed to be in uniform and was in the bullpen watching the action with me. He was a catcher for his summer team and Dusky Baker allowed him to catch bull pens. During the playoffs Dusty let Jason, if needed, warm up pitchers to go into the game.

The call came for Allan Embree and myself to get going, so my son grabbed his mask and glove and warmed me up. I still remember walking through the outfield fence (gate) and looking back at my kid (15 years old) and thinking how cool it was that my son just warmed me up for a Playoff Game! No day of my career compares to that one!

-DOUG HENRY
Pitcher; Milwaukee Brewers, New York Mets, SF Giants, Houston Astros, Kansas City Royals

Winning my first Major League game!

-ED ERAUTT
Pitcher; Cincinnati Reds / Redlegs, St. Louis Cardinals

I had a lot of good days- Enjoyed them all!

-BOBBY RICHARDSON
*Second Baseman; New York Yankees, 8X All-Star, 3X World Series Champion
(Yankees), 1960 World Series MVP, 5X Golden Glover*

I went 4-4 with 2 home runs, a double, and a single scoring, 4 times and drove in 4 runs against the Giants.

-TOM PACIOREK

Outfield / First Baseman; Los Angeles Dodgers, Atlanta Braves, Seattle Mariners, Chicago White Sox, New York Mets, Texas Rangers, 1981 All-Star, Major League Baseball Announcer

My Best Day was May 13th, 1990- the day my daughter Casey was born.

-BILLY BEANE, III
Outfielder; New York Mets, Minnesota Twins, Detroit Tigers, Oakland Athletics, General Manager; Oakland Athletics, 3X Sporting News Executive of the Year, 2x Major League Baseball Executive of the Year

Going into the baseball Hall of Fame, and as a Cardinal was my Best Day.

-STAN "the man" MUSIAL

Outfielder / First Baseman; St. Louis Cardinals, 24X All-Star, 3X World Series Champion (Cardinals), 3X NL MVP, 7X NL Batting Champion, National Baseball Hall of Fame

Best Days:

- Three home runs San Francisco vs. Astros in the Dome
- Making the All-Star Game 3 times and 1 World Series
- God Blessed me with a beautiful mother and father
- God blessed me to play a sport that I loved for 15 years

-JIMMY WYNN

Outfielder; Houston Astros, LA Dodgers, Atlanta Braves, NY Yankees, Milwaukee Brewers, 3X All Star, Houston Astros Hall of Fame

Playing for the Dodgers, when the fans went nuts for my 84 consecutive saves, for "Welcome to the Jungle", the 'Game Over' shirts the fans wore and the best show in town. Those were the Best Days of my life, and I think about them every day.

-ERIC GAGNE

Pitcher, Los Angeles Dodgers, Texas Rangers, Boston Red Sox, Milwaukee Brewers, 3X All-Star, 2007 World Series Champion (Rangers), 2003 NL Cy Young Winner

I signed a pro contract with the Philadelphia Phillies when I was 16 years old – I went directly from American Legion Baseball to the Philadelphia Phillies. I pitched relief in several games, I signed my Pro Contract August 12, 1940 and pitched in relief August 18th.

However, my Best Day in sports was October 3, 1943. I had just turned 17 when I was chosen by the Philadelphia Phillies manager, Freddy Fitzsimmons, to pitch against the Pirates in Forbes Field. This was the second game of a double header. I pitched the complete nine innings and we won the game 11-3. I gave up five hits- I also got a base hit and a RBI. I found out years later that I was the youngest pitcher (17 years and 17 days old) to pitch a complete game and win the game. I am told this is a record that stands today.

-ROGER MCKEE
Pitcher; Philadelphia Phillies

I have been very blessed to have realized every young boy's dream of playing Major League baseball for 8 years and to have played for my favorite team, LA Dodgers, as a young boy growing up.

Also, to continue to be part of Major League baseball for 41 years in the front office and currently as an Advance Scout for the Florida Marlins.

It didn't take me long to realize that no amount of wealth, fame or personal pleasure could fill the emptiness in my life because no matter how much I had it wouldn't be enough. This was all temporary happiness, not lasting contentment and peace. I realized that the key to real joy in life was a personal relationship with Jesus Christ. God was the answer and he filled the void in my life.

My greatest day is the day I accepted Jesus Christ as my Lord and Savior and my journey with Him. My second greatest day is my mother accepting Jesus Christ into her heart hours before she died.

-JOE MOELLER
Pitcher; Los Angeles Dodgers, Scout; Miami Marlins

My Best Day in baseball was 1961 when I signed with the New York Yankees in Grenada MS May 25th, 1961. I flew to New York the next day with Roy Haney, went from the airport to Yankee Stadium. I walked into the locker room and saw Mickey Mantle and Yogi Berra. Moose Skowron shook my hand and welcomed me; they made me feel like I was one of them. I got my picture taken with Mickey and Ralph Houk, I got dressed and went to the field. I just stood there...it was wonderful!

-JAKE GIBBS
Catcher; New York Yankees

My Best Day in life was when my dear wife of 53 ½ years said, "I Do". My worst day was when she passed via cancer in 2009.

Baseball wise: After spending 56 years earning my keep in Major League Baseball, it's hard to single out any particular "Best Days". I had my ups and downs during that time. Being called to the majors at age 21, had to be one of my high points. Getting to play with and against so many of my boyhood heroes. Winning the World Series in 1959 rated high too. One of my favorite moments came in the 1990 World Series—seeing the happiness on the face of catcher Joe Oliver when he drove in the winning run vs. Oakland. (Red's won 4 games to 0). Many other things come to mind, but I have a busy day ahead so I will close off.

-STAN WILLIAMS

Pitcher; Los Angeles Dodgers, New York Yankees, Cleveland Indians, Minnesota Twins, St. Louis Cardinals, Boston Red Sox, 2X All-Star, 1959 World Series Champion (Dodgers), Manager; Boston Red Sox, New York Yankees, Cincinnati Reds, Seattle Mariners, 1990 World Series Champion (Reds)

My first day in "The Bigs" in Boston, 1978.

-WILLIE MUELLER
Pitcher; Milwaukee Brewers

After batting 393 in the Piedmont League, I was sent to Montgomery, AL in the southeast league. Then during the summer of 1950, I was brought up to the Cardinals. My first start in Major League Baseball when Stan Musial was ill, and we were staying in the hotel in Boston.

The managers of the Cardinals, Eddie Dyer, told me I was going to start at first base. I hadn't started in a game for a week and this came to me out of the blue. Dyer said after he went over signs with me that "By the way, Warren Spahn will pitch for the Braves. So, I get my first start against a Hall of Famer.

My knees were knocking against each other and Red Schoendienst came up to me in the dugout and put his arm around my shoulder. He told me he knew I was nervous, but by the 3rd inning the butterflies would be gone. He was right and Spahn beat us 5-0 on a two hitter and I got one of the hits, my first hit in the Big Leagues. Every time I saw Red, I would remind him of his compassion.

-ED MICKELSON
First Baseman; St. Louis Browns, St Louis Cardinals, Chicago Cubs.
September 27, 1953 drove in the final fun in St. Louis Browns history

I knew I wanted to be a baseball play-by-play announcer. When my deal with the Dodgers was finalized, it was the Best Day of my career.

-CHARLEY STEINER

Sports Announcer, ESPN Sports Center, Radio Announcer Los Angeles Dodgers

Curt's two Best Days:
1) The day his best friend, Frank Robinson, assigned me with a job with the San Francisco Giants
2) The Day I said yes to marry him in 1993

We have had no children, just dogs. He was on the road a lot. I am a 29-year retired veteran police officer.

-CURT MOTTON
As told by his wife, Marti Motton
Pitcher; Baltimore Orioles, Milwaukee Brewers, California Angels, 1970 World Series Champion (Orioles), 1967 International League Rookie of the Year, Rochester Red Wings Hall of Fame

I had a wonderful nine-year Major League baseball career that included many memorable days and games. I was surely lucky to be part of the 1969 World Champion New York Mets where I, somehow, made a diving back handed catch of a sinking line drive off Brooks Robinson in the 9th inning of game 4 with the tying and go ahead runs on base. It was a pivotal point in the Series and a catch that is considered by many to be one of the best defensive plays ever in a World Series. The Best Day in my baseball career? No. That was probably earlier in August, when I hit 2 two-run home runs off the Cardinal's Steve Carlton, who was busy striking out a then major league record 19 Mets only to lose 4-3. But even that was not the Best Day I ever had. After my baseball career and during the twenty years spent as a local TV sportscaster, I fell in love with and taught myself something about French Impressionist Art. I collected books on the subject and visited the various Impressionist and Post-Impressionist and early 19th century works in the museums of New York, Boston, Chicago and elsewhere around the United States, dreaming all the while of, one day, travelling to Paris. And so it happened, I went to Paris in the fall of 2002 with my wife and two good friends. I really thought I would burst as we walked the City of Light, Le Ville Lumiere, soaking up the art and architecture. Every minute seemingly filled with meaning and memories that I would never let go of including a very claustrophobic ride up the Eiffel Tower, where, with Paris, like a Christmas garden laid out around us I kissed Cecelia long and deeply. That was a good day, a great day, but not my Best Day.

184

My Best Day ever came during our second trip to Paris two years later with Cecelia and our same two friends. While crossing Pont Neuf Bridge, I first caught sight of the dark, angry clouds, part of a fast approaching storm heading down the Seine towards us from the buildings housing the Louvre and the Musee D'Orsay. The sun was still bright behind us casting a warm glow onto the deep, green trees lining the river against a darkening slate backdrop looming over it all and moving every more quickly our way. That's when I noticed a flock of large, white on white birds stirring and taking flight from the green of the trees along the river's edge. Like all of us avoiding the weather, they launched in stark contrast against a now black sky like light in search of light taking my breath with them as they flew to our left and we raced the other way across the Pont Neuf making it to a sheltering café mostly dry and quickly warmed by a nice bottle of Bordeaux as the big rains hit. I had been moving by so much art that day from the Monets, Turners, and Whistlers atmospheric stuff at the Grand Palais, to the Chagalls, Soutines and Cassatts at the Pompidou and Rodin's statuary breathing in the gardens of his former home. Sweet, magical remembrances all, but strangely and more than a bit surprising, even now, the image that still comes to mind the easiest and lingers the longest from that second trip to Paris is of the day when we were running from a storm and I looked up with the artists eyes and saw those big white birds over the Seine.

-RON SWOBODA

Outfielder; New York Mets, Montreal Expos, New York Yankees, 1969 World Series Champion (Mets

My Best Day was May 20th, 1944. Branch Rickey, General Manager of the Brooklyn Dodgers, came to Buffalo NY (my hometown) to sign me to a Major League contract based on my outstanding records in city league competition. This same league AA caliber produced Warren Spahn, Gibby Sisti, Frank Drews, Danny Ozark, Wally Chipple.

I just concluded the 1943 season, hitting .609, 575 and .495 in three different leagues. I hit 18 homeruns in 22 games, played shortstop, battled clean up, led the leagues in RBI's and hits, and home runs. I joined the Dodgers on the road in St. Louis, and after Leo Durocher looked me over in practice for two weeks. We arrived in Cincinnati to play a four-game series against the Reds. In our first game, Durocher, read off the lineup for the game, with my name at 2nd base. In that game, facing Clyde Shoren, a 6'6" left-handed pitcher who pitched a no-hitter in the game before. In my first at-bat, on the 2nd pitch I smashed a triple off the left center field wall. On that hit, I set a record, a 10-million-to-one odds accomplishment. It was republished in "Ripleys believe it or not" that I went from the amateur league, directly to the majors, something that was never done before. We won the game 6-1, I handled seven chances with a double play. I am the only player in the history of baseball who went directly to the Major Leagues without ever playing in High School or the minors. This was no fluke and it was my Best Day.

-EDDIE BASINKSKI
Infielder, Brooklyn Dodgers, Pittsburg Pirates

My Best Day in the Big League would have to be my first game. I beat the Washington Senators 7-3. I pitched the whole game, struck out Roy Sievers three times who was quite a hitter. I also hit a 3-run homer right out of Fenway Park. The first guy to greet and congratulate me was the great Ted Williams. Big thrill for me.

-JERRY CASALE
Pitcher; Boston Red Sox, Los Angeles Angels, Detroit Tigers

My Best Day in Baseball is when I went to spring training with the Washington Senators in Orlando, Florida in 1955, and put on the major league baseball uniform and ran onto the field to take infield and batting practice; it was my boyhood dream that came true!

-MICHAEL DANTE

Actor / Shortstop; Boston Braves, Washington Senators

Being in baseball for 38 years gave me so many Best Days. A few of those memories:

- Playing against Joe Di Maggio and Ted Williams in 1941
- Hitting a home run in Yankee Stadium in 1945
- Hitting against Bob Feller in my first major league game in Washington was no fun because his fast ball was clocked at 110-112 miles per hour! He beat us 2-0 and struck out 17. It was scary facing him with no helmets

I have many more memories of the era I played in, but those are the highlights.

-HILLIS LAYNE
Third Baseman; Washington Senators

The question about my "favorite sports day", in retrospect and after many others over a long period if time has led me to believe that there is not one day that I can put at the top.
I have come to what I think is a reasonable answer, that being that the whole experience of baseball; from the sandlot, American Legion, Clemson College, minor leagues and briefly in the Major Leagues all combined for my "Greatest Day".

I was just very fortunate to have had the opportunity to do this. My son Bill had six plus years in the Major Leagues (mostly with the Pirates) gave my wife and I some great moments as well.

-JOE LANDRUM
Pitcher; Brooklyn Dodgers, 1952 National League Champions

It was August 1986, and I was playing AAA ball for Denver who was affiliated with the Cincinnati Reds. We were in Oklahoma City playing the AAA Texas Rangers. After the game a group of us went out for a few pops. When Mike Konderla (my road roommate) and I got in it was about 2:30am. The red light on the phone was flashing so I called to retrieve the messages. I had two. The first was from my Mom- it simply said to call her ASAP! The second was from Jack Lynn, our manager and it simply said call me ASAP. As I sat on the edge of the bed, ears ringing from the buzz kill, I gathered myself and thought the worst. I was busted for curfew and much worst perhaps something bad had happened back home. Maybe my Dad had a heart attack! My parents live in South Carolina, so it was about 5:00 am EST. Mom answered the phone and told me the bad news, My best friend and neighbor growing up was killed in a car crash earlier that day. I was devastated. After I regrouped, I figured I might as well get the second phone call out of the way. A sleepy Jack Lynn answered and in a mean voice said, "GET DOWN TO MY ROOM RIGHT AWAY". I went down to his room expecting to get fired for missing curfew. I knocked on the door and Jack opened it. Standing in his boxer shorts, looking mad, Jack broke out into a huge smile and handed me an envelope. He simply said, "CONGRATULATIONS- YOU ARE GOING TO THE BIG LEAGUES!"

-BILL LANDRUM
Pitcher; Cincinnati Reds, Chicago Cubs, Pittsburgh Pirates, Montreal Expos

191

My Best Day was my first win in the majors. It was the first time I was on the mound.

-FRANK BAUMANN
Pitcher; Boston Red Sox, Chicago White Sox, Chicago Cubs, 1960
AL ERA Leader

- World Series 1981
- 1981 playoff game win over Oakland
- 1987 World Series

-GEORGE FRAIZER
Pitcher, St. Louis Cardinals, New York Yankees, Cleveland Indians, Chicago Cubs, Minnesota Twins, 1987 World Series Champion (Twins)

My Best Day was game 163 of the 1980 baseball season. We had to play an extra game to decide the division championship vs Los Angeles Dodgers. I went 3-5 with a homerun and 4 RBI's and Joe Niekro won his 20th game 7-1.

-ART HOWE

Infielder; Pittsburg Pirates, Houston Astros, St. Louis Cardinals, Manager; Houston Astros, Oakland Athletics, New York Mets, Coach; Texas Rangers, Colorado Rockies, Texas Rangers, 1981 Player of the Month

What a story of determination, I salute you!

My Best Day was the first day in Brooklyn 1956,
putting on a Major League uniform. My first impression
was seeing the players I had read about in the dressing
room in their Dodger uniforms. I was given #27. That
night Sal Maggie pitched a no-hitter against the Phillies.
My first at-bat was not good, I was so thrilled just being
there I didn't swing the bat and struck out. Though I
pinch hit and my first swing in The Majors was a home
run in Ebbetts Field, my boyhood dream had come true!
I had the privilege of playing with 6 future Hall of
Famers: Jackie Robinson, Duke Snyder, Pee Wee
Reese, Sandy Koufax, Don Drysdale, and Roy
Campanella.

-DON DEMETER
*Outfielder; Brooklyn / LA Dodgers, Philadelphia Phillies, Detroit
Tigers, Boston Red Sox, Cleveland Indians, 1959 World Series
Champion (Dodgers)*

One of my Best Days was when my dad left a bow strung in his Archery shop in Chicago. I took the bow and proceeded to put an arrow in the dining room door. When my dad told my mom "it's time for him to start shooting.", I was only two years old. When I was 12 my brother Joe came to me and said let's tell dad we want to play baseball instead of archery. My dad said that if one of us won the Nationals in archery that year we would be allowed to play baseball. We won the Nationals and my mom & dad lived long enough to see my brother and I sign a contract with the Los Angeles Dodgers and a pitcher / catcher combo in 1961. Going to Spring Training and meeting Joe Campanella and realizing that he knew more about catching and baseball than I would learn in a lifetime. I was only up for a cup of coffee, but my brother went on to play for nine years with the Dodgers.

Another Best Day would be the day I watched polo players riding at Huntington Beach Equestrian Center I asked them how do you get started and from that day forward I have been actively playing polo for the past 18 years. I have also been the President of Pacific Coast Polo Club, and a certified umpire & delegate with the United States Polo Association.

-GARY MOELLER
Catcher, Los Angeles Dodgers

It has nothing to do with baseball, but my Best Day happened while at a stadium in 1982 in Medford Oregon. I was in a chapel service and the Chaplain spoke from the bible and explained God's plan of how to go to Heaven when we die. He explained how our sins has separated us from God and that the only way to Heaven was to trust Him.

-KEITH HUGHES

Outfielder; New York Yankees, Philadelphia Phillies, New York Mets, Cincinnati Reds

I find that most of my great memories of baseball are in the people I met. Roger Maris threw out a runner for me at home plate to save a 2-1 win in the 1956 World Series.

I remember that in my twilight years of baseball I was working out with the Los Angeles Dodgers, and Jerry Lewis used to come out and practice with us. He loved the game, wanted to be a ball player but had two-left feet.

When I played in the Pacific Coast League, Frank Lovejoy hardly missed a game. I was given almost 19,000 1964 AuraVision baseball records from a fan that I still have most of them.

From time to time great stories come to mind, and I smile.

-JOHN GRAY
Pitcher, Philadelphia Athletics, Kansas City Athletics, Cleveland Indians, Philadelphia Phillies, Rollins College Hall of Fame

I can remember a day against the Chicago White Sox where I hit a couple of home runs and had 7 RBI's.

-DICK GERNERT

First Base / Left Field; Boston Red Sox, Chicago Cubs, Detroit Tigers, Cincinnati Reds, Houston Colt .45, 1961 World Series (Reds)

"Best Day in baseball" for players not being long-term major-league players usually boil down to 3 things:

A) Signing the pro contract
B) Reaching the major league
C) First hit or first win

Since doubling in my first at bat (as a pinch hitter) meant I had achieved "B"- the double in my first at-bat would rank as my Best Day in baseball.

Being employed 52 consecutive years in the game, you can see where picking one would be very difficult.

-STEVE DEMETER
Third Baseman; Detroit Tigers, Cleveland Indians, Scout / Minor League Manager Pittsburg Pirates

My Best Day was in 1950. It was opening night of the baseball season. I was the 3rd baseman for the Brooklyn Dodgers, and we were playing the Phillies

A childhood dream come true!

-BOBBY MORGAN

*Third Baseman; Brooklyn Dodgers, Philadelphia Phillies,
St. Louis Cardinals, Chicago Cubs*

When the Dodgers picked me up from the Twins in 2018, it was my happiest day. I am getting a fresh start, a second chance. This place is crazy, man. Being at camp is awesome. Looking at this place, it is so bright and merry. Even when I was playing catch yesterday, I was like, "the ball is so light, why is everything so light and fluffy here?" I am thrilled!

-J.T. CHARGOIS

Pitcher; Minnesota Twins, Los Angeles Dodgers

My Best Day is everyday that I smile to myself and am thankful
for the love of my family

-SANDY ALDERSON

*General Manager, New York Mets, San Diego Padres, Senior Advisor to
Baseball Operations, Oakland A's. 2015 Baseball American Executive of the
Year Award*

Outside my family, there were four Best Days, in no particular order:

- My sophomore year at UCLA 1938. I started at end in the season-opening football game against Iowa, which we won. My dad, who had broken his back, came to my game in an ambulance and was propped up on the sidelines to watch.
- In late October of 1955, John Galbreath, owner of the Pittsburgh Pirates, announced my appointment as General Manager. I succeeded Branch Rickey, one of the great men in Baseball history.
- October 3, 1960 at 3:35 PM Bill Mazroski's home run in the bottom of the ninth in the 7th game of the World Series defeated the New York Yankees 10-9. It was Pittsburgh first championship in 35 years. The Yankees bombed us in their three victories, 16-3, 10-0 and 13-0. Our four wins in the series were nail-bitters. Gino Cimoli, our top outfield replacement, shouted in the clubhouse "they broke all the records, but we won the series" The city of Pittsburgh went wild.
- While the 1960 series victory was my first, and a memorable thrill, our defeat of Baltimore 2-1 in the deciding game on October 17, 1971 was even more meaningful to me. My predecessors had left 11 men who played prominent roles in our 1960 victory.

-JOE L BROWN

General Manager; Pittsburgh Pirates, 2X World Series Champions (Pirates)
5 NL East Division Titles

Winning game 5 against the Cubs to get the Dodgers to go to the 2017 World Series is a dream come true. For me, to hit a grand slam and a total of 4 home runs for my guys, the team…so far this has been my Best Day ever.

-ENRIQUE "KIKI" HERNANDEZ
Utility; Houston Astros, Miami Marlins, Los Angeles Dodgers, 2017 & 2018 National League Championship

I had many Best Days catching Sandy Koufax and Bobby
Shantz, and Virgil Trucks. Putting on my uniform every day
was a Best Day, too.

-CHARLIE THOMPSON
*Catcher; Brooklyn Dodgers, Kansas City Athletics, Detroit Tigers, Coach; St.
Louis Cardinals, Scout; St; Louis Cardinals, Los Angeles Dodgers, Baltimore
Orioles*

As I reflect back on all of the wonderful things that have come my way due to the fact that I could play a little baseball, my Best Day might surprise you. It's not going to be any day during the 1984 World Series where I hit .412 with 2 home runs and had 7 RBI's and was named the Padre's MVP. It's not going to be any one of the day's in 1977 where I hit .333 for the season and was a valuable part of the Texas Ranger's pennant drive. Nor is it going to be any one of all the wonderful day's I spent in professional baseball after the 1st day I reported to play for the Tampa Tarpons in the Florida State League, I originally signed with the Cincinnati Reds and reported to the Reds single A affiliate in the Florida State League on June 21st, 1967 where I was surrounded by outstanding baseball player's from all walks of life. Black, white and Latin from the North, the South and foreign countries. I found out very fast that I wasn't the best, or even one of the best like I was used to being and that I had to work hard to earn my spot. I also learned very fast to respect the game, my peers, and my coaches and I will be respected in return. June 21st, 1967 was my "Best Pro Baseball Day".

-KURT BEVACQUA

Infielder; Cleveland Indians, Kansas City Royals, Pittsburgh Pirates, Milwaukee Brewers, Texas Rangers, San Diego Padres.
1984 World Series (Padres)

My Best Day was in 1958 when I was playing for Colorado Springs. In Des Moines, Iowa I was asked by my manager to pitch the second game of a double header because of illnesses of other members of our staff. I had had only a two-day rest following a game in which I had "gone the distance" in. I agreed to give it a shot. The result was a No-Hitter, and if my memory serves me well, there wasn't a ball hit out of the infield the entire game.

My Best Day memory, overall, was my first appearance in a regular season major league game. That hundred-yard walk from the bullpen to the mound literally felt like it took an eternity to get there. It still gives me chills when I reflect on it.

-HAL TROSKY JR.
Pitcher; Chicago White Sox

It would be very difficult for me to pick one Best Day. I have a number of them: when I married my wife Cheryl, and the birth of my son Brian, daughter Lauren and my other son Timmy were all incredible days.

From a Cardinals perspective, October 27th, 2006 was one of the Best Days in my time with the Cardinals, representing the culmination of all we work towards. That morning, we announced a deal to build Ballpark Village and that evening we won our tenth World Championship at home in the ballpark we christened just six months earlier. It was a magical day, full of joy and fellowship a day I won't soon forget.

-MARK LAMPING
President, St. Louis Cardinals

The 2013 wildcard game against the Reds, I can still feel the energy from that night!

-NEIL WALKER

Second Baseman / First Baseman; Pittsburgh Pirates, New York Mets, Milwaukee Brewers, New York Yankees, Miami Marlins, 2014 Silver Slugger Award, Participated in the first-ever MLB 4-5-4 triple play, May 9, 2015

One of my Best Days was pinch-hitting for Willie McCovey and driving in the tying run, the runner was Willie Mays!

-JOEY AMALFITANO

Second Baseman / Third Baseman; New York and San Francisco Giants, Houston Colt .45s, Chicago Cubs, General Manager Chicago Cubs, Coach; San Francisco Giants, San Diego Padres, Cincinnati Reds, Los Angeles Dodgers, 1988 World Series Champion (Dodgers)

June 11th, 1983 was my Best Day in baseball because I faced off against my hero, Johnny Bench. I was so nervous, and Johnny knew it by the way my legs were trembling. (I was 19-years old). He said, "kid, just see the ball and swing at it". I did…I struck out. I went 0 for 2 but we won the game. An Awesome Day.

-ALBERTO GILBERTO "GIL" REYES

Catcher; Los Angeles Dodgers, Montreal Expos. 1988 World Series Champion (Dodgers)

As far as baseball is concerned, my Best Day was throwing a four-hit shutout in game 4 of the 1997 NLCS when I was with the Braves vs the Marlins. We were down two games to one and we needed the win big time. I felt like I couldn't do anything wrong that night. I was definitely in the proverbial "zone" that night.

As far as personally, hands down it is a tie between the day my oldest son was born, and the day my boy & girl twins were born.

-DENNY NEAGLE

Pitcher; Minnesota Twins, Pittsburgh Pirates, Atlanta Braves, Cincinnati Reds, New York Yankees, Colorado Rockies, 2X All-Star, 2000 World Series Champion (Reds), 1997 NL wins leader

Today is my Best Day!
Yesterday is part of my memory.
Tomorrow is in the planning.

I pray that God helps me into tomorrow to enjoy a fullness of life and duty but today he has a hold of my hand as I see, hear and feel the present.

The breathes I took yesterday are gone but today treasured. To feel the soft fur of my pet and hear the birds start to sing as I watch the sun come up are only happening right now, today.

Tomorrow may bring adjustments but today is in the moment. I just smelled the breakfast cooking and heard the leaves rustle and saw my dog chase a squirrel. The peach I am experiencing right now is priceless. Yesterday was great and I pray tomorrow brings new joys but right now, today, I love what is happening.

Today I can try to change some things that happened yesterday and plan some for tomorrow…but today I will try to carry out what I planned yesterday.

Today is my Best Day!

-JERRY KOOSMAN
Pitcher; New York Mets, Chicago White Sox, Philadelphia Phillies, 2X All-Star, 1969 World Series Champion "Amazing Mets", Mets Hall of Fame

My Best Day in baseball:

Playing in two games of the 1960 World Series for the Pittsburgh Pirates against the Yankees in Yankee Stadium and winning both games. We Finally won the series on Bill Mazeroski's home run in the 7th game.

-BOB OLDIS

Catcher; Washington Senators, Pittsburgh Pirates, Philadelphia Phillies, 1960 World Series Champion (Pirates), Scout; Miami Marlins

It is a tie:

- Five hits and 2 home runs against the San Francisco Giants
- Two home runs and 3 RBI's against Sandy Koufax in a 4-3 Cub victory over the Los Angeles Dodgers

-GEORGE ALTMAN

Outfielder; Chicago Cubs, St. Louis Cardinals, New York Mets, 3X All-Star

Greatest day was the 1978 Yankee's World Series victory and the 1981 World Series vs. the Yankees while playing on the Dodgers when I pinch-hit the go ahead home run to win the game off Ron Guidry

Billy Martin was the best Manager; Tommy Lasorda was more fun and the best to play for.

-JAY JOHNSTONE

MLB Outfielder, Anaheim Angels, Chicago White Sox, New York Yankees, Los Angeles Dodgers, 2X World Series Champion (Phillies / Dodgers)

In High School, those days they didn't draft you. They approached you. if the team liked you, the problem with that in the old days was that if you signed over 4K you went straight to the major leagues with no experience. Only about 5 or 6 guys would do that. Killebrew, Koufax, Al Kaline, etc. did that. I was signing out of high school and I wanted experience. I was approached by the New York Yankees, Dodgers, Cincinnati & Philly-no draft. I worked out with them-and the Yankees said I could workout with them during home stands. I got to hit with the big guys, Yogi Berra, Mickey Mantle, Bobby Richardson, Elston Howard, Moose Skowron, Whitey Ford-and I worked out. Malcom Patterson from the Dodgers came by too. Malcom found out I was going to sign with the Yankees on a Tuesday night, he had Jackie Robinson call me the Sunday night before the Yankees wanted me to sign Tuesday night. I signed Tuesday afternoon with the Dodgers!

-TOMMY DAVIS

Left Field / DH, LA Dodgers, NY Mets, Houston Astros, Oakland A's, Chicago Cubs, Anaheim Angels, KC Royals, 3X All-Star, 1963 World Series Champion (Dodgers), 2X NL batting champion

Mr. Williams has had many memorable Best Days. I guess if you are looking for one of them it would be the day he was inducted into the Hall of Fame. It really meant a lot to Ted to be placed among the best baseball players and some of his dearest friends. Some other (Best Days) would be related to days spent fishing.

-TED WILLIAMS
Left Fielder; Boston Red Sox; 19X All Star, 2X AL MVP, 6X AL batting champion, 4X home run leader, National Baseball Hall of Fame (Dictated by Ted to Donna Fleischmann, personal assistant)

My Best Day was when we won our first World Championship in 1966 against the Los Angeles Dodgers.

-BROOKS ROBINSON

Third Baseman; Baltimore Orioles, 18X All-Star, 2X World Series Champion (Orioles), 1964 AL MVP, 16X Golden Glover, Baltimore Orioles Hall of Fame and #5 retired, National Baseball Hall of Fame

Game six of the 1995 World Series.

-GREG MADDUX

Pitcher; Chicago Cubs, Atlanta Braves, Los Angeles Dodgers, San Diego Padres, 8X All Star, 4X NL Cy Young Winner, 18X Golden Glover, 1995 World Series Champion (Braves), Atlanta Braves Hall of Fame and #31 retired, National Baseball Hall of Fame

I think my very Best Day was in 1972 in the playoffs against Pittsburgh. Johnny Bench hit a home run in the 9th inning of the 5th game to tie it. We went on to win in the 9th.

-SPARKY ANDERSON

Second Baseman; Philadelphia Phillies; Manager; Cincinnati Reds, Detroit Tigers, 3X World Series Champion (2X Reds / 1X Tigers), 2X AL Manager of the year, Cincinnati Reds Hall of Fame and retired #10, National Baseball Hall of Fame

The 1972 playoffs against the Pittsburgh Pirates. I hit a home run in the 9th inning of the 5th game to tie it and went on to win the game in the 9th. Also, my retirement game, I hit a home run.

-JOHNNY BENCH

Catcher, Cincinnati Reds, 14X All Star, 2X World Series Champion, (Reds) 2X NL MVP, 10X Golden Glove Award, Cincinnati Reds Hall of Fame & #5 Retired, National Baseball Hall of Fame

Here's what I would consider my Best Day: I was playing Little League in 1967. My dad was sitting in a lawn chair straight-away, center field, behind the fence. I came up to bat, hit my very first ever home run right into my dad's hands. That was my Best Day ever. I still have that baseball prominently displayed in my home.

-BUCK SHOWALTER

Manager; New York Yankees, Arizona Diamondbacks, Texas Rangers, Baltimore Orioles, 3X AL Manager of the Year

My Best Day would have to be the day I left the Indian River Hospital in Vero Beach, Florida after a stay of four months, including six weeks in critical condition in intensive care due to a traffic accident.

That day, July 24, 1990 is my best day because my doctors told my wife that I had only an eight percent chance of surviving the second surgery.

-JAMIE JARRIN

Spanish Broadcaster; Los Angeles Dodgers, National Baseball Hall of Fame

The best day of my life would be October 22, 1980 the
date of the parade down Broad Street to old JFK
Stadium to celebrate the 1980 Championship
Philadelphia Phillies.

To witness the hundreds and thousands of fans lined up
the length of Broad Street to the overflowing 100,000-
seat JFK Stadium was breathtaking. It was a true love-
in of Philadelphia fans and their championship team. I
was honored to emcee the ceremonies at JFK Stadium.
Philadelphia fans are known to be tough, but on this
day, it was truly a love affair of a city's only World
Championship baseball team and an entire city's
wonderful baseball fans.

-HARRY KALAS

*Baseball Announcer, Houston Astros, Philadelphia Phillies, Ford C
Frick Award*

Every day I put on a baseball uniform was my Best
Day.

-GENE MAUCH

*Infielder; Brooklyn Dodgers, Pittsburgh Pirates, Boston Braves,
Chicago Cubs, Boston Red Sox, Manager; Montreal Expos,
Minnesota Twins, California Angels, 1981 AL West Division
Champions*

October 3, 1951: Giants-Dodgers playing for the pennant. Last of the 9th inning, Dodgers are winning 4-2. One out, 2 men on. I got up and hit "the shot heard 'round the world" to win the pennant 5-4.

-BOBBY THOMSON

Outfielder; New York Giants, Milwaukee Braves, Chicago Cubs, Boston Red Sox, Baltimore Orioles, 3X All Stars, 1969 NL Pennant, Staten Island Sports Hall of Fame

I have had a blessed life and feel like every day is my Best Day. Giving my life to Jesus Christ when I was 9-years old was my best day! Getting married to my wife was next, then the birth of my children were wonderful days! Signing with the New York Yankees at 17-years old wasn't that bad either!

-REX HUDLER

Utility Fielder; New York Yankees, Baltimore Orioles, Montreal Expos, St Louis Cardinals, California Angels, 1999 Fresno Athletic Hall of Fame Announcer; Los Angeles Angels of Anaheim, Kansas City Royals

The day I got my own locker and Major League uniform with my name on it; it was a day my prayers, as a kid, were answered.

-JOHNNY VANDERMEER

Pitcher; Cincinnati Reds, Chicago Cubs, Cleveland Indians, 4X All- Star, 3X NL Strikeout leader, pitch two straight no-hitters on June 11 & June 15th, 1938, 1940 World Series Champion (Reds), Cincinnati Reds Hall of Fame

In 12 seasons with the Dodgers our team played in 6 World Series so there were many great days. My very best was in 1953, October 2nd against the Yankees-- winning 3-2 on a homerun by Campanella in the 8th. I had 14 strikeouts--a World Series record. Among them was Mantle 4 times, and the final, Johnny Mize, a great hitter.

-CARL ERSKINE

Pitcher, Brooklyn/ Los Angeles Dodgers, 1954 All Stars, 1955 World Series (Dodgers)

My Best Day was being on the mound October 1, 1967 when the Boston Red Sox won the American League Pennant at Fenway Park. We beat the Twins 5-3 and 30,000 people came on the field to celebrate the victory.

-JAMES LONBORG

Pitcher, Boston Red Sox, Milwaukee Brewers, Philadelphia Phillies, 1967 All Star, AL Cy Young Award, 1967 AL Win Leader & Strikeout Leader; Boston Red Sox Hall of Fame

My Best Day--Saturday, June 14, 1962 versus the New York Yankees in Cleveland Stadium. My fourth hit that day was a two-run homerun in the last of the 9th that won the game 9-8. That victory in front of 65,000 fans tied the Indians for the American League lead with the Yankees.

-JERRY KINDALL

Second Base; Cleveland Indians, Chicago Cubs, Minnesota Twins, Coach, University of Arizona; 4X College World Series Champion

Really a tough question to ask; I always thought my days were good. Just putting on the Major League uniform every day of the season were the Best Days. One series in Boston over a weekend I drove in 14 runs, hit some homers, and had a good weekend. One day in Washington I hit my 6th straight home run in 6 straight games to tie the American League record. It took 17 innings, but I did it off Al Aber of Detroit. Had a wonderful career; wouldn't change anything.

-ROY SIEVERS

First Base / Outfield; St. Louis Browns, Washington Senators, Chicago White Sox, Philadelphia Phillies, 5X All-Star, 1949 AL Rookie of the Year, 1957 AL Home Run Leader & AL RBI Leader

Driving in the winning run 1975 World Series in the 9th inning.

-JOE MORGAN
Second Base; Houston Colt .45, Cincinnati Reds, Houston Astros, San Francisco Giants, Philadelphia Phillies, Oakland Athletics, 10X All-Star, 2X World Series Champion (Reds), 5X Golden Glove Award, 2X NL MVP, Cincinnati Reds Hall of Fame & #8 retired, National Baseball Hall of Fame

Max tells me his Best Day was when he joined the Cleveland Indians in 1946. Lou Boudreau signed him for an exhibition game against the Indians. When he joined in '46 as first base coach, it was great. In Cleveland Stadium where 80,000 people honored Babe Ruth, Ty Cobb and Tris Speaker, he had the honor of shaking hands with these immortals.

He performed for two innings of every baseball game to standing ovations and stayed on for 1946 and 1947.

Max has had to retire this year, (1995) much to his dismay; for baseball has been his life. After 50 years it isn't easy to say goodbye.

-MAX PATKIN
baseball entertainer (as told by his sister, Ruth Cohen)

My Best Day on the baseball field would be difficult to categorize. One that stands out in my memory is the first time I hit my 50th home run in 1947. It was a goal I never dreamed possible in only my second year in the Major Leagues, especially since I had just three home runs at the end of May that year.

-RALPH KINER

Outfield; Pittsburg Pirates, Chicago Cubs, Cleveland Indians, 6X All-Star, 7X homerun Leader, New York Mets Hall of Fame, Pittsburgh Pirates #4 retired, National Baseball Hall of Fame

My best day was game five of the 1964 World Series. In the 10th inning I hit a three-run home run to win the game.

-TIM McCARVER

Catcher, St. Louis Cardinals, Philadelphia Phillies, Montreal Expos, Boston Red Sox, 2X All-Star, 2X World Series Champion (Cardinals); St. Louis Cardinals Hall of Fame, MLB Announcer

Every day when I wake up, I cherish every moment.

-VIDA BLUE

Pitcher; Oakland A's, San Francisco Giants, Kansas City Royals,
6X All-Star, 3X World Series Champion (A's), 1971 AL MVP & AL
ERA Leader, No-Hitter September 21, 1970, San Francisco Giants
& Oakland A's Hall of Fame

My Best Day--I would probably have to say it would be getting the last out in the 7th game of the 1972 World Series.

-ROLLIE FINGERS

Pitcher; Oakland A's, San Diego Padres, Milwaukee Brewers, 7X All-Star, 3X World Series Champion (A's)
, 1981 AL MVP & Cy Young Winner, Oakland A's Hall of Fame & #34 Retired, National Baseball Hall of Fame

The 1951 World Series--Giants versus Yankees. I got
four straight hits and stole home for the first time in 30
years. When I came up for the fifth time, I lined out to
Joe Collins, the Yankees' first baseman; the ball was hit
really hard and Joe was lucky to catch it.

-MONTE IRVIN

*Left Field; New York Giants, Chicago Cubs,1952 All-Star, 1951 NL
RBI Leader, 1954 World Series Champion (Giants), San Francisco
Giants #20 Retired, National Baseball Hall of Fame*

My Best Day: paying back my parents for college
tuition.

-MARK PRIOR

Pitcher; Chicago Cubs, 2001 Golden Spikes Award, 2003 All-Star

My Best Day was in September 1975 when I won my 20th
game in San Diego against the Dodgers.
I was the first Padre to ever win twenty games.

-RANDY JONES

*Pitcher; San Diego Padres, New York Mets, 1976 MLB win leader, NL Cy
Young Winner, 2X All-Star, San Diego Padre's Hall of Fame & #35 Retired*

Hitting a home run in the 1943 All Star Game, we won 5-3 in
Philadelphia.

-BOBBY DOERR

Second Base, Boston Red Sox, 9X All-Star, 1943 World Series (Red Sox),
Boston Red Sox Hall of Fame & #1 Retired, National Baseball Hall of Fame

1963 - Marrying Diane.
1967 - First Major League game with Detroit.
1985 - Broadcasting Pete Roses' 4,291st hit.
1990s - The wedding days of our daughters and birth of four grandchildren.

-DAVE CAMPBELL

Infielder, Detroit Tigers, San Diego Padres, St Louis Cardinals, Houston Astros ESPN Sportscaster

My Best Days were the days my kids were born. The Saturday night I hosted my first Sports Center was also exciting. I'd worked on ESPN2 for several months and wanted the chance to prove I could do the "big show." I'd set the goal of doing *Sports Center* as a teenager. Accomplishing that was a big kick.

-RECE DAVIS
ESPN Sportscaster

The days I made it to the Big Leagues. That opening day,
with all those people yelling.

-MARK FIDRYCH

*Pitcher; Detroit Tigers, 2X All-Star, 1976 Rookie of the Year, 1976 AL ERA
Leader*

My wife and I will be married 52 years come this January 1997.
Perhaps that was my Best Day.

-JOHNNY PESKY

Short Stop / Third Base; Boston Red Sox, Detroit Tigers, Washington Senators, 1946 All-Star, Boston Red Sox Hall of Fame & #6 Retired; MLB Manager, Boston Red Sox

My Best Day was winning the World Championship in 1981. It was a culmination of hard work and determination over the years.

-RON CEY

Third Base, Los Angeles Dodgers, Chicago Cubs, Oakland A's,
6X All-Star, 1981 World Series MVP & Champion (Dodgers)

There have been so many blessed days in my life, and God has been so good to me that it is difficult to choose one. But if pressed to do so, I will say it was June 17, 1961. That was the day I was married to my wife of now more than 43 years, Lin. We met on a blind date and played miniature golf while the proprietor sang hymns in the background. One year later, we wed in an early morning ceremony, in the garden of my parent's home. I was 22 and Lin was 20.

-ROSS PORTER

MLB Announcer, Los Angeles Dodgers

I have had a lot of remarkable good days, but I believe the Best Day I ever had was the day I brought major League Baseball back to Milwaukee. I've had some remarkably great days since then but the thrill of returning Major League Baseball to Milwaukee and Wisconsin will always be the ultimate Best Day for me.

-ALLAN H. "BUD" SELIG

Commissioner of Major League Baseball, National Baseball Hall of Fame

I assume you mean my Best Day in broadcasting. It came in the 1969 Winter Olympics at Squaw Valley when the U.S. Hockey Team defeated the Russians for the first time and I also won the gold medal. It was one of the most emotional days I can recall.

I have always felt that the 1960 team did not receive enough recognition they accomplished the feat 20 years before the 1980 hockey team won.

-LON SIMMONS

San Francisco MLB Announcer; recipient of the Ford Frick Award

I had some great days, a lot of them. To pick out one would be hard. In the 1942 World Series, 1946 World Series, and 1956-57-58 Series with the New York Yankees.

-ENOS SLAUGHTER

Right Field; St Louis Cardinals, New York Yankees, Kansas City Athletics, New York Yankees, Milwaukee Braves, 10X All-Star, 4X World Series Champion (2X Cardinals / A's / Yankees), 1946 NL RBI Leader, St. Louis Cardinals Hall of Fame & retired #9, National Baseball Hall of Fame

Winning the World Championship. A veteran player obtains goals, achieves status and money, but the ultimate goal is to win a championship.

-DARREN DAULTON

Catcher, Philadelphia Phillies, Florida Marlins,
3X All-Star, 1992 Silver Slugger Award, 1992 NL RBI Leader, Philadelphia
Phillies Wall of Fame, 1997 World Series Champion (Phillies)

My Best Day? Every day!

-ERNIE BANKS

Short Stop / First Baseman; Chicago Cubs, "Mr. Cub",
14X All-Star, 2X NL MVP, Gold Glover Award 1960, 2X NL Home Run
Leader, Chicago Cub Retired #14, Major League Baseball All-Century Team,
National Baseball Hall of Fame

I've had lots of Best Days; difficult to pick just one…birth of children and grandchildren…meeting my wife, Mary Ann Montanaro, and being on the 1982 Cardinals when we won game seven of the World Series…many days watching great racehorses and playing great golf courses.

-JIM KAAT

Pitcher; Philadelphia Phillies, New York Yankees,
St. Louis Cardinals; 3X All-Star, 16X Gold Glove Award, Minnesota Twins
Hall of Fame, 1982 World Series Champion (Cardinals)

First day in the Big Leagues- all my dreams came true.

-BRONSON ARROYO

Pitcher; Pittsburg Pirates, Boston Red Sox, Cincinnati Reds, Arizona Diamondbacks, 2006 All-Star, 2004 World Series Champion (Red Sox), 2010 Golden Glove Award

With regards to my storied baseball career, if the reader is a baseball fan the answer is obvious. It would be the October day in 1977 when I hit three home runs on three successive pitches in the World Series, taking the New York Yankees to the championship and winning the Most Valuable Player Award. I would like to pass along a thought-provoking quote, "unless you try to do something beyond what you have already mastered, you will never grow." I truly believe that my Best Day is yet to come and hope that you will strive to make every day your Best Day.

-REGGIE JACKSON

Right Field, Kansas City/ Oakland Athletics, Baltimore Orioles,
New York Yankees, Anaheim Angels, 14X All-Star,
5X World Series Champion (3X A's / 2X Yankees), 2X World Series MVP,
1973 AL MVP, 4X Homerun Leader, Oakland A's Hall of Fame and #9
retired, New York Yankees #44 Retired, National Baseball Hall of Fame

My Best Day as far as USC goes was being inducted into the USC Sports Hall of Fame, this was May 3, 2002.

-STEVE KEMP
Left Field, Detroit Tigers, Chicago White Sox,
New York Yankees, Pittsburgh Pirates, Texas Rangers, 1979 All-Star

My Best Day was July 9, 1976 when I no hit the Expos. Didn't get to sleep until 6:00 A.M. A close second was the day we clinched the Central Division Championships in my rookie year as manager, 1997.

-LARRY DIERKER

Pitcher; Houston Colts/Astros, St Louis Cardinals, 2X All-Star, July 9, 1975 pitched a no-hitter, Houston Astros Hall of Fame and #49 Retired, MLB Manager; Houston Astros, 1998 NL Manager of the Year

If it is pertaining to Sports, from the Bull Pen to pitch in Yankee Stadium. I had 2 outs and 2 runners on base, Mr. Mantle was the batter. 60 thousand in the stands. I got him to strike out!

-BILL LEE

Pitcher, Boston Red Sox, Montreal Expos, 1973 All Star, Boston Red Sox Hall of Fame

I know my father's "Best Days" are right now. He was the best father anyone could wish for. He has all my awards, and I know there are rewards for that. Good luck with your book.

-JOHNNY LOGAN

Shortstop; Boston/ Milwaukee Braves, Pittsburgh Pirates, 1957 World Series (Braves), 4X All-Star, Miller Park Walk of Fame
(As told by his son, John Logan Jr.)

I have had many great moments in my seven years in baseball. One of the great things was making so many good friends. One exciting moment was winning the Eastern League Pennant on the last day of the season. I pitched the game in New York for my eighteenth win. Of course, I will never forget the first game of the year against the Orioles. I was called on in relief to come in with the bases loaded to face Frank Robinson. My knees were shaking. I hit him in the back with my first pitch. And, of course, I made my one and only start two weeks later in Kansas City. Those are just some of my Best Days.

-PETE MAGRINI
Pitcher, Boston Red Sox

My Best Day in baseball was the day my mother saw me play for the first time at Dodger Stadium. That is a day I will never forget.

-DAN NORMAN
Right Field, New York Mets, Montreal Expos

My "Best Day" was elongated over a full baseball season- 1961

That was the year Mickey Mantle and Roger Maris chased 'The Babes' record of 60 home runs. Of course, Roger broke it with 61.

I was fortunate to bat 2nd that season, behind Bobby Richardson and before Roger and Mickey. The climax was a World Series Championship in 5 games!

-TONY KUBEK

Shortstop; New York Yankees, 4X All-Star, 3X World Series Champion (Yankees), 1957 AL Rookie of the Year, Canadian Baseball Hall of Fame, Baseball Announcer; announced 12 World Series

If there is one accomplishment for which I am particularly proud of, it is that I've always served baseball to the best of my ability. Never have I deliberately done anything to discredit the game, the Tigers or my family.

-AL "Mr. Tiger" KALINE

Right Field, Detroit Tigers, 18X All-Star, 1968 World Series Champions (Tigers), 10X Golden Glove, 1973 Roberto Clemente Award, Detroit Tiger #6 retired, National Baseball Hall of Fame

My Best Day in Baseball was when I was called up to the Big Leagues to the Giants at the Polo Grounds. The field was breathtaking. I was 24 and I pitched 9 innings against the Phillies, we won 6-0! My second game was against the Dodgers at Ebbets Field and we won 6-0! It was record breaking and thrilling!

-AL WORTHINGTON

Pitcher, New York / SF Giants, Boston Red Sox, Chicago White Sox, Cincinnati Reds, Minnesota Twins, Alabama Sports Hall of Fame

To sum up what was my Best Day there could be several.

- The day I signed a pro contract in August 1934
  - My 1935 season
  - My 1936 season
  - My 1937 season
- My 1944 start with the Chicago White Sox as an outfielder against the New York Yankees at Yankee Stadium.
- Getting to fill a dream of being able to play in the Major Leagues

As I look back to 73 years ago (93 years-old in 2009), the 1935-1937 seasons gave me the test I still cannot believe, and it took 3 years for my Best Day to happen.

1935 my first year in Oklahoma I played in the class C western association as a 19-year-old left-handed pitcher. I won 20 games, lost 11 and started 32 games, 29 completed games and relieved 3 other games. I won 3 games for the Championship and also got credit for winning the All-Star game. What a great year for a rookie, little dreaming what was in store for me in the 1936 season.

268

I was recalled at the end of 1935 to the Los Angeles Angels Club for Spring training. I injured my arm in a pepper game, I locked arms with a fellow player and pulled the deep muscles in my throwing arm. It caused so much pain and I was sent back to Oklahoma to get rehabilitated for the year.

My arm was not healing, or the shoulder and I lost 10 games in a row. I couldn't

believe what was happening to me: in the 2nd inning of the 10th game, I was taken out in the 2nd inning, 10 runs behind. Mike Gazella, the Ex-Yankee utility player was our manager and instead of sending me to the club house he put me in right field. I replaced Lynn Socath, who was leading the league in hitting. Here is where I finished that game.

Remembering only the booing and cat calls from the fans. My hometown fans calling for my transfer elsewhere.

-ED CARNETT

Pitcher / Left Field; Boston Braves, Chicago White Sox, Cleveland Indians

My Best Day was signing my first contract at a try out in Milwaukee for the Boston Braves. I was signed by Jake Flowers, the GM for AAA team May 8, 1947

-BERT THIEL

Pitcher, Boston Braves, Manager, Kansas City Athletics, Chicago White Sox

The Best Day of my life was when I married my wife of 44 years, Anna. Our extended family of 3 sons, 4 grandchildren to date, have made life worthwhile.

-PETE VUCKOVICH

Pitcher, Chicago White Sox, Toronto Blue Jays, St. Louis Cardinals, Milwaukee Brewers, 1982 AL Cy Young Award, 1981 AL win leader

My Best Day was when Connie Mack came to our farm in Sanford, NC and signed me to a professional contract in 1948. I was the last player, or one of the last players, Connie Mack signed.

Another Best Day was in 1950 when I came in as a relief pitcher and faced Al Rosen, Ralph Kiner and Larry Doby with no outs and the bases loaded; Cleveland failed to score! I got a standing ovation from 35,000 fans.

-BILL HARRINGTON
Pitcher, Philadelphia / Kansas City Athletics

My Best Day in baseball was Opening Day in 1948 at
Fenway Park, Boston when I stepped on the field.

My dream came true!

-BILLY DE MARS

*Short Stop, Philadelphia Athletics, St. Louis Browns, Assistant
Coach Philadelphia Phillies, Montreal Expos, Cincinnati Red, 1980
World Series Champion (Phillies)*

Right now, at the age of 99 years-old and the 2nd oldest living baseball player, every day I wake up to the sunrise, hear the birds chirp, and see another sunset, is my Best Day.

I have had an active life over the years. I played baseball and football until Ted Williams told me to stop playing football and concentrate on baseball.

I was in the service, a LA country sheriff during the Watts riots and escorted Charles Manson to court each day of his trial, and a champion horse trainer.

The absolute Best Day of my life was hearing that the war had ended, and I got to go home!

-GEORGE ELDER
Outfielder, St. Louis Browns

The first time I put on the Dodger uniform, and every day after that when I would put on my uniform for a game.

-TIM THOMPSON

Catcher, Brooklyn Dodgers, Kansas City Athletics, Detroit Tigers, Coach St. Louis Cardinals, Scout, Los Angeles Dodgers, St. Louis Cardinals, Baltimore Orioles

I have three Best Days:

1) Being called up to the Big Leagues by the Cardinals
   2) I hit for they cycle in a game. I had 3 singles, 1 double, 1 triple with 6 hits and one strike out. When we went into extra innings, I tried as hard as I could for a home run and got it!
3) My first hole in one in golf. I have had 12 total, but the first one was very exciting

-LEE TATE
Shortstop; St. Louis Cardinals

My Best Day was when the Boston Red Sox called me up to the Major Leagues in 1957. A dream come true, which every young man has a dream of playing baseball in the Major Leagues.

-KEN ASPROMONTE

Second Base; Boston Red Sox, Washington Senators, Cleveland Indians, Los Angeles Angels, Milwaukee Brewers, Chicago Cubs, Manager; Cleveland Indians

My Best Day was the first home run I hit in the majors,
a Grand Slam against the San Francisco Giants.

-BOBBY MALKMUS

*Infielder, Milwaukee Braves, Washington Senators, Philadelphia
Phillies, 1957 National League Pennant, 1959 Sports
Writers MVP Award*

My Best Day in baseball was when I met Virginia Lee Pullen in Wichita Falls, Texas and she said "yes". She wanted to marry me! Baseball was my stepping-stone to Texas where I met the love of my life. I survived World War II and the Korean War, we have been married 59 years, 2 months, and 22 days (as of 6/24/20).

-FRANK SAUCIER

Outfielder; St. Louis Browns, 1950 Minor League Player of the Year
San Antonio Missions

Going 4-5 off Bob Gibson in 1960 was my Best Day. The Giants Juan Marichal was the winning pitcher in the game.

-HOBIE LANDRITH

Catcher; Cincinnati Reds, Chicago Cubs, St. Louis Cardinals, San Francisco Giants, New York Mets, Baltimore Orioles, Washington Senators, First ever pick of the New York Mets in the 1961 MLB expansion team, Coach; Washington Senators

I was a pinch hitter for St. Louis and hated it. Spring training in 1953 I hit a home run over the center field fence in Memphis. It was over 3 fences, over 500 feet.

By the way, I have 12 children. I think the most of any ball player ever.

-LARRY MIGGINS
Outfielder; St. Louis Cardinals

One day I'd gone 15 innings pitching. Top of the 15th, and this old boy hit a homerun on me. The temperature was in the 90's that say. We lost the game, 1-0. After the game, a sportswriter came up to me. He saw the whole thing. He asked me, "what happened out there?" I said, "some you win, some you lose, and some get rained out."

-JIM WILLIS
Pitcher, Chicago Cubs

Being called up from the minor leagues to the St. Louis Cardinals near the end of the 1952 season was pretty heady business for a 20-year-old St. Louis native. To be playing on the same field as my baseball heroes like Stan Musial and Red Schoendienst was definitely an ego booster. However, that didn't last long when on my way from the clubhouse to the dugout I encountered two young teenagers asking for my autograph. Graciously I stopped and signed their scorecard. As I walked away, I heard one boy ask the other, "who did you get?". He replied "Neal Hertweck". The second boy brought be back to earth quickly when he said, "Who the heck is that?"

The two days I played in Major League games were the Best Days of my baseball career.

-NEAL HERTWECK
First Baseman; St. Louis Cardinals

I've had a fabulous career as a player and a coach in the Major Leagues. I had some great years in San Diego with the Padres! My Best Day would have to be when we were playing Boston. I had warmed up 7 times the night before in the bull pen but didn't get in the game. I was sure I would get the day off. Ha Ha! I was entered the game in the 2nd inning to face "The Yaz" with the bases loaded and 2 outs, down 3-0. I got him out on a little bouncer to the mound to save all the runs. I hit a home run in my 1st at bat. In my 2nd at bat, I hit a base-hit to left field. George Case, the 3rd base coach, had me stealing 2nd base as Jim King hit a single to right field over my head as I was running and I scored all the way from 1st on a base hit to right with a great slide at home plate. The score then was 3-2. My arm was hanging and my whole body was tired, but they sent me out to pitch another inning. That should have never happened, but it did. I gave up a couple weak hits and walked a man and ended up hurting my arm before I got out of the inning. My arm was hurt the rest of the year and I was finally returned to Cincy and went to San Diego at the end of July. My Best Day turned out to be the day that ended my Major League career. I never made it back to the Major Leagues even after 2 great years in San Diego Coast League and 2 MVP awards.

-RAY RIPPELMEYER

Pitcher, Washington Senators, Coach, Philadelphia Phillies

Hitting two-run homer in the top of the 22nd inning to win longest game in Yankee history.

-JACK REED

Outfielder; New York Yankees, 1961 World Series Champion (Yankees)

After living 90 years on this earth it would be hard for me to pick one event. Instead, I'll have to give you a choice:

1) When I proposed to my wife, VaNita. We have been together now as a married couple 70 years. She has really been the glue in our family as with a professional baseball player, I'd be away from her and the family a long time, 154 games from February to the middle of October. While I was gone, she ran the ship of 5 boys and 1 girl. There was always crises that came up with broken bones, cuts on fingers, toes and schedule of activities they had took her in two directions at the same time. Living in Meridian, Idaho, presented even more challenges resulting in driving across the country when there were no freeways to get the family back in time for school. She was always organized so she could be in the right place at the right time. She was a Super Woman and was responsible for my having a successful career.

2) When I got called up to the Big Leagues after 2 years in the minors. It was a thrill to put on a Big League uniform and compete against some of the greatest players during the era of the game. I had a 2-year service time in the Army during the Korean Conflict. I went into the service in 1951-1953 back in Dt. Eustis, Virginia. We had our firsts child born in the hospital on base for $7.50. Our lives were in constant change and, thanks to my wife, she hung in

there so I could continue my career. 1960 came and we had a great year. I mean every one of us put our hearts and soul into every game and we came away winning the National League Championship. So the next challenge was the New York Yankees who were heavy favorites. Las Vegas lost of money as we beat them in a 7 games series, 4-3.

3)   Another Best Day was when I was named the starting pitcher in the 1st game of the World Series in 1960, which we won. Then the Yankees hammered us the next two games, but Harvey Haddix won his game in New York. I won the following game in New York and we returned to Pittsburgh for game 6 and 7. I knew game 7 was all on my shoulders. I pitched well enough to win that game also but going into the 7th inning I had a 5-2 lead, but got into a bit of trouble with 2-men on and 1 out. Our manager decided to bring in our closer and he threw up a 3-run homer and the Yankees had a 5-run inning to go ahead. We came back and had a 5-run inning as well giving us a 2-run lead. At the top of the night 9th, Bob Friend was brought in and the 1st 2 hitters got base hits and he was taken out of the game. Haddix was called on and before he got them out, they had tied up the game 9-9. Being the home team, we had one mor at bat. Mazeroski was our hitter and on the 2nd pitch he tags a homerun for a 10-9 victory and a World Series Championship. That home run put Mazeroski in the Hall of Fame

and I won they Cy Young Award for the best
pitcher in baseball.

I had an even better year in 1965, but because
our team didn't play well for me, we didn't make it
back to the World Series. In 1967 I decided to hang
up the glove, work at Idaho National Bank, and
enjoy my family.

The years passed and I was 70, then 80, and now 90
years old. I can't believe it as I've lost all my
family before they turned 70, so I am living on
borrowed time.

Now, for my Best Day ever, which came after the
worst day ever. My wife and I were sitting down to
have spaghetti and meat ball dinner when my wife
got up from the table to get something at the
counter in the kitchen. I said, "Honey, come and sit
down so we can eat" and she didn't answer me, so I
got up and went over to her. I cold see something
was wrong, she mumbled something, but I couldn't
understand on word she said. It was a a stroke, a
blood clot in the brain. I called 911, and she spent 3
weeks in the hospital, we gave her a Priesthood
blessing from our son, Vance, and asked the Lord to
protect her. We asked for a miracle and we got one
as the doctor who handles these cases tried to get
the clot but was unable. After giving up, she
received medicine to soften the clot to pass out of
her system. At that point, we were given the no
hope for a full recovery. Vance asked the doctor 4

questions: 1. Will she recognize people? 2. Will she be able to eat or swallow? 3. Will she be able to walk again? 4. Will she any quality of life? All of the answers were "no". So that evening our daughter and I went in to say our final good-bye to her. We knelt down beside her and had 15 minutes with her- that's all the time they would allow us to stay because of the COVID-19 virus. We told her how much we loved her and needed her so please don't give up. We had prayed and asked the Lord for a miracle. She didn't open her eyes or say a word to us, but we got a slight nod of her head. The doctors & nurses thought it was out good-bye, but the next morning she showed improvement and began to communicate with us. The staff then worked with her. We couldn't visit her again, but we would call morning and night to talk with her, to facetime her. With encouragement, she made 3 weeks go faster and has since been able to come home, walk, talk, and eat but most importantly be with us still.

The very Best Day of my life.

-VERN LAW

Pitcher, Pittsburgh Pirates, 2X All Star, 1960 World Series Champion, 1960 Cy Young Winner

My Best Game was against the Boston Red Sox, I went 3 for 4 with a homerun, ripple, and a double with 6 RBI's and we won 12-11.

Best Day? When I was called back to Washington from Chattanooga.

-JERRY SNYDER
Short Stop / Second Baseman; Washington Senators

My Best Day is really My Best Days. Each time my name was used in a baseball conversation, radio, articles since I was first to be a ball player it was "Don Lee, son of Thornton Lee". My father was a Major League pitcher with Cleveland and Chicago White Sox for 14 years. Really, it was used a lot and each time was my Best Day.

-DON LEE

Pitcher; Detroit Tigers, Washington Senators / Minnesota Twins, Houston Astros, Chicago Cubs

I'm 86 now (2020) and every day, when I get out of bed looks like it will be my Best Day, even though there are many things I can no longer do.

I have been very fortunate; I have had a lot of Best Days. Oh, there were some that were disappointing, but on a balance of things, they do not outweigh the good days.

Two of my Best Days were when my two boys got into college: Kenny, the older one, into Wesleyan and the younger one, Geoffrey, got into Yale. Two very good days.

-KEN MACKENZIE
Pitcher; Milwaukee Braves, New York Mets, St. Louis Cardinals, San Francisco Giants, Houston Astros

My Best Day was June 10th, 1959 in Baltimore when I hit 4 consecutive home runs for the Cleveland Indians.

-ROCKY COLAVITO

Right Field / Left Field; Cleveland Indians, Detroit Tigers, Kansas City Athletics, Chicago White Sox, Los Angeles Dodgers, New York Yankees, 9X All-Star, 1959 AL Home Run Leader, 1965 AL RBI, 1st AL outfielder to play a complete season with a perfect 1,000 fielding percentage, Leader, Cleveland Indians Hall of Fame

I have a few Best Days:

1) My first contract ever! Was I excited!
2) The first time in the Major Leagues for the rookie- me!
3) I out-played two different pitchers for a spot in San Francisco's line up by facing and winning against the Hall of Fame hitter, Billy Williams, with a weak pop up; struck Ernie Banks and Ron Santo. I won the game, so off the San Francisco.
4) Willie Mays received an all time honor at home plate of the Polo Grounds by 50,000 fans for twenty minutes. "The hair on my head stood straight up"

-JOHN PREGENZER

Pitcher; San Francisco Giants

My Best Day was playing in 2 1962 MLB All-Star Games. (MLB has 2 All-Star Games from 1959-1962) I was born in a textile village in Montgomery, AL in 1933 in the midst of the "Great Depression".

After 10 years of minor league and military service, here I was playing with so many "legends of Baseball". Guys like Mickey Mantle, Roger Maris, Yogi Berra, Luis Aparicio, and Bill Skowron. On the opposing NL team was Willie Mays, Don Drysdale, Stan Musial, Ken Boyer, Robert Clemente and others. I had 1 hit in each game. I was the first Angel ever to get a hit in an All-Star Game. I was also the first American Leaguer to hit a homerun in Chavez Ravine (AKA Dodger Stadium)

-BILLY MORAN

Second Baseman; Cleveland Indians, Los Angeles Angels of Anaheim, 2X All-Star

My greatest thrill was my first start, that was in June of 1956 against the Brooklyn Dodgers. I pitched a 2-hitter and beat them 8-1.

-DON KAISER

Pitcher; Chicago Cubs

My Best Day in baseball was the day of my only Major League win in Chicago, when I was with the Dodgers in 1958. The thing I remember most was that the plate seemed wider than it had ever been during my career. I kept asking my catcher, John Roseboro, if those pitches that were being called strikes were really over the plate? He said, "Absolutely. You're throwing in the zone where I'm setting up. If you do that all the time, the umps with give you those pitches."

To which I replied, "Those pitches are balls in the minors. I guess I've been pitching in the wrong league."

It was also interesting to be relieved by Johnny Podres with 2 down in the eighth inning. I had two strikes on Dale Long, a left-handed hitter, when I bounced a curve ball through the legs of Roseboro. It would have been OK, except that the runner on first moved to second in scoring position. The score was 2-1 in our favor. Alston came out of the dugout like a shot and replaced me with Podres. I argued that I wanted to stay in. I said that I've struck him out twice today and I know I can do it. Roseboro also tried, saying "Skip! It was my fault. I should've blocked it". It was no use.

Podres came in, threw one pitch for strike three and we were out of the inning. He finished the ninth, and the game. Roseboro brought the ball to me as a souvenir. It's now in my trophy case labeled "First Big League win". Obviously, I expected a few more, but it was not meant to be.

It was still my Best Day.

-RALPH MAURIELLO
Pitcher, Los Angeles Dodgers

My Best Day was in 1961 when I was purchased from the Indianapolis Indians by the Twins. I joined the Twins in Cleveland and played my first game in that Stadium. A great thrill after spending years in the Minor Leagues.

One other Best Day was when I hit my only home run off of my ex-teammate, Don Rudolph (Also a good friend)

-RUSS SNYDER

Outfielder; Kansas City Athletics, Baltimore Orioles, Chicago White Sox, Cleveland Indians, Milwaukee Brewers, 1966 World Series Champion (Orioles)

My Greatest Day was putting on a Major League uniform and staying for 16 ½ years with the Major Leagues.

If you are looking for my other good days, I have a few.

August 19th. 1958 in Cincinnati I hit 3 home runs in one game, tying a record of a lot of other players.

On August 1-2-3, 1962 I hit 2 home runs in 3 straight games for a total of 6 home runs.

July 8th, 1961 I had another Best Day where I made baseball history. I was with the Milwaukee Braves when we as a team hit four homeruns in succession in one inning by four different players. This was the first time this was done in all of baseball history. Eddie Mathews hit the first homerun in the 7th inning in Cincinnati off of pitcher Jim Maloney, Hank Aaron hit the second homerun off of Maloney. They changed pitchers and brought in Marshall Bridges. Joe Adcock hit the third homerun off of Bridges and I, Frank Thomas "The Original One", made baseball history by hitting the fourth homerun!

-FRANK THOMAS
Left Field / Third Baseman / First Baseman; Pittsburg Pirates, Cincinnati Reds, Chicago Cubs, Milwaukee Braves, New York Mets, Philadelphia Phillies, Houston Astros; 3X All-Star

My Best Day was winning the 7th game of the 1962 World Series 1-0 in San Francisco and being named World Series MVP. Especially after losing the 7th game of the 1960 World Series.

-RALPH TERRY

Pitcher; New York Yankees, Kansas City Athletics, New York Yankees, Cleveland Indians, 2X All-Star, 2X World Series Champion (Yankees), 1962 World Series MVP, 1962 AL wins leader

I have had a few Best Days:

1) There was a baseball writer, David Halverstadt, who
wrote a book about my teammate, Curt Flood. David
called me to asked if I knew Curt Flood, and if I had
read Curt's autobiography? Curt talked about how badly
he was treated in the south, lots of bigotry, where he
had to separate himself from the white boys, he couldn't
eat in the same restaurants and things like that. Curt
mentioned me in his book, saying, "There is a white
boy from Knoxville, TN by the name of Buddy Gilbert,
who would go into restaurants and bring us food on the
bus to make sure we could eat when we were travelling
on the road. Buddy treated me like a human." I cried,
that was the nicest compliment. Mr. Halverstadt got me
in contact with Curt, and I got him on the phone
(pretending to be mad) saying "How dare you use my
name in your book?" He was thrilled to have me call
and we had a great talk.

2) 1954 was my first year in pro baseball. One of our big
pitchers, George McCloud, came up to me and put me
down, saying I was a God Damn N*&#@ lover. I just
looked up at him and told him he was not born that way,
someone taught him to hate and if he would read the
Bible he would not have such hate. George never got on
me again.

3) Hitting my first homerun in Cincinnati was another Best Day. I was so excited. A writer from the paper said I ran so fast the cameras couldn't keep up with me.

4) Back in the day, Roberto Clemente was tagged as having the best arm in baseball. A friend called me to see if I was watching the ball game where the announcer just said Roberto had the best arm. He knew that in 1959 I beat Roberto in a throwing contest. Pittsburgh put up Clemente, and Freddie Hutchins put me up in a hitting/throwing contest. I beat him in all 3 bases, where I won money too. Roberto said, "Hey kid, you have one helluva arm". Roberto Clemente was team player, a manager's player and was not only out for himself but played for the team and the fans. Beating a future Hall of Famer was my highlight.

-BUDDY GILBERT
Outfielder; Cincinnati Reds

My Best Day in baseball was playing in Minneapolis, the triple A team for the Boston Red Sox when I had three homeruns and a triple for the four times I was at bat. Of course, I was also very fortunate to play in the Majors. I played pro ball for ten years!

-DON GILE

First Baseman / Catcher; Boston Red Sox

I have 5 kids and each of their births were something to remember, of course.

Jim, the third one, was born over two months premature. Because his lungs were not developed, the doctor said he wouldn't make it. However, after a month in an isolation and another month in an incubator, he did make it! Thanks to the great nuns, nurses, and doctors at Nazareth Hospital in Philadelphia.

The day he came home some of my teammates, friends, and family had a great party. Nobody left before dawn. Later that day we played the Braves. Even with the extensive hangovers, I think we won by about ten runs.

"My Best Day" – knowing Jim was okay and also besting the National League champs by about ten runs when most of us had trouble navigating!

-TED KAZANSKI
Short Stop; Philadelphia Phillies, Coach; Detroit Tigers

Since I played behind an MVP shortstop and Hall of Fame second baseman I didn't have too many memorable moments. Dick Groat won the MVP award after he was traded to the Cardinals in 1963. My roomies Bill Mazeroski, the best pivot man I ever saw, was later voted into the Baseball Hall of Fame.

Here are a few incidents that I recall from my brief Major League career:

- Our spring training was held in Fort Meyers, FL back in those days and segregation was the law of the land. On a bus trip back from an exhibition game in Clearwater, I remember going into a café and bringing a sandwich to Roberto Clemente because they wouldn't serve him.
- During spring training Maz and I were awakened in the middle of the night by the hotel manager telling us we had to evacuate the building because there was a fire. It turned out to be minor, but you still couldn't see through the smoke.
- I tripled off Vern Law in an inter-squad game and Frank Leary (Detroit) in an exhibition game. Both times the next at bat they knocked me down and struck me out.

- The first time I saw Forbes Field, Groat suggested that Coach Danny Murtaugh hit us some ground balls. Dick said the infield was too rough and went back in, I stayed and the first ground ball took a dirty hop and hit me in the face. The first thing I saw when I finally looked up was Murtaugh doubled over, laughing at me. I had a black eye for a week.
- One of the first regular season games I played in was against the Brooklyn Dodgers. It was a national TV "Game of the Week" broadcasted by Leo Durocher. In the ninth inning I pinch ran for Frank Thomas. I was thrown out by Carl Furillo trying to go from first to third on a Billy Virdon single to right field. I was running with my head down and ran through the 3rd base coach's stop sign. That ended the game and to this day I am still embarrassed by that base running blunder. Joe Brown, our general manager, came right into the shower room to see what I was thinking.
- My first Big League at-bat was against Milwaukee. I pinch-hit a line drive against Taylor Phillips, which I thought was a tweener for a sure double. Bill Bruton, their center fielder, came out of no where to make the catch.

- It was so cold that I couldn't feel my feet running to first base.

- My first start was against Brooklyn and I got my only hit against Don Newcombe, which contributed to our win. I also made my only error in that game. I tried to throw around Gil Hodges who came in standing up on a double play. A couple of innings later Charlie Neal tried the same thing, but I leveled him to complete the double play.

- In Philadelphia one day, Maz and I slept in and were late to the park for a day game because I thought it was at night. Our club house called us when they discovered we weren't on the bus to the ballpark. Fortunately, we got there in time for infield practice.

- One day a blond crawled over the low wall at Wrigley Field and sat down next to me while I was sitting on the bench in our bullpen. She never said anything and just waited patiently for the ushers to come and take her away.

- I was thrown out of the last game of my Big League career! They set me up. I was going into the Army the next day and somebody gave me a real going away present. While I was

308

- sitting in the corner of our dugout, minding my own business, I heard in a loud voice, "YOUR OUTTA HERE"! I looked around and saw the umpire pointing at me. I meekly got up and went in and took a shower. In retrospect, I wish I would have gone out and put on a show. We could have a lot of fun with it.

I spent 45 years in professional baseball as a player, manager, or scout and cherished every moment of it.

-BUDDY PRITCHARD

Short Stop / 2nd Baseman; Pittsburgh Pirates, Coach Pirates Minor League; Scout, Chicago Cubs

My Best Baseball Day was in the 1964 World Series. The Cardinals vs. The Yankees. I pinch hit and started the inning off. Later Ken Boyer hit a bases loaded home run to put us one run ahead. We ended up beating the Yankees!

-CARL WARWICK

Outfielder; Los Angeles Dodgers, St. Louis Cardinals, Houston Colt 45s, Baltimore Orioles, Chicago Cubs, 1964 World Series Champion Cardinals (Cardinals)

The greatest experience of mine being in the Major Leagues was going to the park each day and watching all the great players and the great things that happen during the games.

This amusing thing happened to me at a reunion at MSU a few years ago- a group of guys from the team asked me what it was like to pitch to Mickey Mantle.

My first time went like this:
1st pitch to Mantle was a swing and a miss
2nd pitch was a slow curve fouled off
3rd pitch was a fast ball right down the middle of the plate and the umpire said, "ball 1". I was furious. We went on and finally I got him out.

As I was coming in the umpire said to me, "Ed you know that 3rd pitch was a strike. But the people came here to see Mantle hit. I knew it was going to be tough after that. I loved every day of my career.

-ED HOBAUGH
Pitcher, Washington Senators

My Best Day was my 1st day in the Major
Leagues with the Washington Senators.

At age 28 and after 6 outstanding years in the
minors, I never thought I would get to my
dream. I had a great start, and was going good
until bone chips in my pitching elbow along
with a botched surgery ended it all.

No regrets. The Lord got
Me there, and I couldn't ask for more.

-DAVE STENHOUSE
Pitcher; Washington Senators, 2X All-Star

Man, I admire you. I went through 6 hernia and 4 knee operations, with an aortic valve replaced from my hip bone. But, you, Mark make me look like a piker

I had 2 good days:

1) I pitched a 14-inning complete game but lost 1-0
2) I won a double header and I pitched 7 innings in the 1st game and relieved 2 innings in the 2nd game for another win.

-TED WIEAND
Pitcher; Cincinnati Redlegs/Reds

The Best Day of my life was when Jesus Christ became Lord of my life.

In baseball, being selected to the 1960 All-Star team.

-DICK STIGMAN

Pitcher; Cleveland Indians, Minnesota Twins, Boston Red Sox, 2X All-Star

My Best Day Ever:

I grew up in Philadelphia, PA in the forties and fifties. In June 1951, I graduated from Olney High School where our varsity baseball team had just won the High School Championship in baseball. I was part of that team and had just received a scholarship to Lafayette College in Eaton, PA. I wanted to become a civil engineer.

A few weeks later, I attended a baseball camp near my home held by Jack Coombs and Ira Thomas, two ex-Major League players. I learned later that Jack was the baseball coach at Duke University in Durham, NC. I do not remember who talked to whom, but I was offered a baseball scholarship to Duke. I am sure my dad was behind the change.

So, in September 1951 I boarded a train from Philadelphia to Durham to start my college education. Therefore, I believe that day in June 1951 was my Best day.

Why?

1953 April: I met my wife to be, Patricia Ann Tarleton
June: Duke was one of eight teams to attend the College
World Series. I was named to the baseball All-
American Team.

1954-June: I signed with the Milwaukee Braves to play
pro baseball.

1955-February: I married Patricia Ann and went to my
first Spring Training Camp, which led to the births of
my son, David, and my daughter, Laura.

1962- February: I was sold to Houston where I have
lived with my family ever since.

So, without that day in June, 1951, none of the above
would have happened.

-AL SPANGLER

*Outfielder; Milwaukee Braves, Houston Colt 45s, Houston Astros,
LA/California Angels, Chicago Cubs, drove in the first run in
Houston Colt 45s history*

Memorial Day, 1955 the Chicago Cubs played the St Louis Cardinals in St. Louis. We played the Cards in a double header. I hit a home run in the first game that won the game. In the second one, I also hit a home run to win that game too!

I grew up in Springfield, MO where most were Cardinal fans and my desire was to be able to play for the Cards, of course. However, I was offered a contract with Chicago. so I became a Cub in 1948. My career was interrupted by Uncle Sam and I spent 2 years in Japan but was able to play ball at Camp Drake outside of Tokyo. My Rookie year was 1955.

My mom and dad came up to St. Louis for the double header which made it extra special.

-BOB SPEAKE
Outfield; Chicago Cubs, San Francisco Giants

I am proud that I was a good Major League player to be able to hang around for almost seven years and to coach for the Royals for 8 seasons.

As a player in the Cardinal organization in St. Louis in 1961-1962, and when I played, I usually hit 6th behind Stan Musial. My first base hit was a line drive to center field after Stan Struck out. My 1st home run was a grand slam off Jim Brewer and Stan Musial was the first to meet me at home plate to shake my hand, I always thought Stan Musial was not only a great player but a really great person.

Another thing I'm proud of is that when I was managing in the Baltimore Orioles system, I had Eddie Murray in AA Ashville. He struggled at times and I approached him and had him hit left-handed (he was right-handed) just to get a different feeling at the plate. I used to do that when I was a player. Just getting comfortable. We remained good friends and he always reminds me that a lot of people claim changing him, but he always says "you and I know".

-JIM SHEFFER
Catcher; St. Louis Cardinals, Chicago Cubs, Chicago White Sox, New York Mets, Philadelphia Phillies, Cincinnati Reds

The Best Day I ever had was February 16, 1957 when I married my wife which was 63 years ago.

The Best Day I ever had in baseball was probably the first pitch I threw as a Major League pitcher. This was in 1961.

Also, one day against the Cincinnati Reds I threw a little over 80 pitches in a 9-inning game. This was probably the Best Day I had in Major League Baseball.

Baseball was good to me and my family.

-JACK CURTIS
Pitcher; Chicago Cubs, Milwaukee Braves, Cleveland Indians

My Best Day happened prior to my 16 years in Professional Baseball, which included 10 years with the Chicago White Sox, Then 3 years with the Boston Red Sox, an American League Rookie of the Year Award in 1963, a 20-win season in 1964 and two All-Star selections (1964 & 1967).

My Best Day was being able to play first base with my father Tom at second base in the summer of 1955, before my final year of High School.

My father was an avid Yankee fan his entire life, played semi-pro baseball until the age of 48 and passed away due to ALS.

-GARY PETERS
Pitcher; Chicago White Sox, Boston Red Sox, 2x All-Star, 1963 AL Rookie of the Year, 1964 AL win leader, 2X All-ERA leader

My Best Day, other than my marriage, was in 1961. As a rookie with the Cincinnati Reds, I got a chance to play in the 1961 World Series against the New York Yankees.

-JOHNNY EDWARDS

Catcher; Cincinnati Reds, St. Louis Cardinals, Houston Astros, 3X All-Star, 1963 & 1964 Golden Glove Award

My Best Day was when I met my wife in 1958. She has been my mate and my best friend for 61 years. Now, more than ever, I need her more and I am so glad I have an incredible partner.

-ED BRESSOUD

Shortstop; New York / San Francisco Giants, Boston Red Sox, St. Louis Cardinals; 1964 All-Star, 1967 World Series Champion (Cardinals)

My Best Day!

1964 Cleveland pitcher was Sonny Seibert, bases loaded. Fastball, fouled off!

Was Manager Mr. Lipez going to have someone pinch hit for me?

NO!

Another fastball. BAM! Grand Slam! McNertney's first and only!

-JERRY MCNERTNEY

Catcher; Chicago White Sox, Seattle Pilots, Milwaukee Brewers, St. Louis Cardinals, Pittsburg Pirates

You sound as if you had a very tough time, and you are looking for "Best Days" is very interesting, a great idea.

I had a few Best Days. The day I married my wife, and the day we had our only child, were two great days.

In Baseball, I had a few that stand out for me. I was a rookie in 1963. MY team, the Los Angeles Dodgers, played the New York Yankees in the World Series. I played and faced Whitey Ford in the first game. In the second inning I singled to center off him. My father and most of my family was there. We swept the Yankees in four games; it is hard to top that.

-DICK TRACEWSKI

Infielder; Los Angeles Dodgers, Detroit Tigers; World Series Champion, (2X Dodgers / Tigers) Coach / Manager; World Series Champion (Tigers)

Like most good days in our lives, it is the result of a history of events that culminates in a most memorable experience; a day that one will never forget and is so powerful that it can even influence how we live the rest of our lives.

For me, that day came in August 1958.
As a youngster, I was encouraged by my aunts, who played in women's baseball leagues in the 1930's, to play baseball. When I was four years old my aunt Vi gave me a baseball glove and my journey began.

Growing up in Penticton, BC, Canada, there was no organized baseball leagues. As a result, I started pitching for a semi pro team at the age of 15. I had good success, including striking out batters in one game. This drew the attention of some professional baseball scouts and I was drafted out of high school in 1954 by the Boston Red Sox. I played for their minor team, the San Francisco Seals, On my fourth pitching start of the season I dislocated my ankle sliding into second base and was out the rest of the year. I was very disappointed and worried that I may have lost an opportunity to make it to the Big Leagues.

In 1957 I was called up to the Big Leagues by the Red Sox. Also called up was my roommate, Bill Monbouquette and teammate Bud Byerly. This was an exciting and scary time. Meeting the Big Leaguers, including the great Ted Williams (who turned out to be a wonderful teammate) and signing my first Big League contract for $8,000 with the owner, Tom Yawkey. He made me feel at home and made signing a Big League contract with the Red Sox truly a day I'll never forget.

As great of a day as that was, there was more to come. In my first appearance, I was asked to pitch the ninth inning against the Detroit Tigers. I was so nervous I can't remember anything about my outing or who I faced. All I can recall about the games is Jim Bunning, pitching for the Tigers, threw a no-hitter against us.

In August 1958 we traveled to New York to play the Yankees. This was the first time I saw Yankee Stadium. There I was, in my Red Sox uniform, standing in the dugout looking out at the venerable park, with so much history represented by the statues in center field and the pennants hanging from the façade. I was impressed and in awe.

To make the experience even more incredible, I noticed who was taking batting practice at the time; Number 7, the great Mickey Mantle. The ball just sounded different coming off his bat, like nothing I'd ever heard before. Mantle was followed by Roger Maris and Yogi Berra in the batting cage. Legendary players right before my eyes!

On this road trip, I got my first start in the Big Leagues, pitching against Bobby Shantz and the Yanks. We won the game, 7-2. What a thrill to beat the Yankees in Yankee Stadium. It doesn't get any better than that!

-TED BOWSFIELD

Pitcher, Boston Red Sox, Cleveland Indians, Los Angeles Angels, Kansas City Athletics

In 1962, I held the record of 57 consecutive error-less games by a 3rd baseman. That year, and being inducted into the Houston Hall of Fame, were my Best Days.

-BOB ASPROMONTE

3rd Baseman; Brooklyn / Los Angeles Dodgers, Houston Colt .45's, Atlanta Braves, New York Mets; Holds Houston's record of Grand Slams (6), Houston Astros Hall of Fame

Best Day:

1960 -Star Game in Kansas City

-BUD DALEY

Pitcher; Cleveland Indians, Kansas City Athletics, New York Yankees, 4X All-Star, 2X World Series Champion (Yankees)

My Best Day:

First win and first hit against the Dodgers

-BOB DULIBA

Pitcher; St. Louis Cardinals, Los Angeles Angels, Boston Red Sox, Kansas City Athletics

My Best Day? Not one but many:

- Football scholarship to get into Syracuse University 1957
- Meeting Ginny at Syracuse, she is now my wife of 59 years
- Three great children
- Five years in the Majors- First hit and first homerun that Hall of Famer Steve Carlton gave up in1965
- 3 consecutive pinch hit doubles (Major League record)
- Proud that I achieved a BS & MS at Syracuse
- 36 years as VP of Sales & marketing following baseball
- 7 wonderful grand children

My Best Day could be my Best Life. I have been blessed with great health and happiness. I truly believe that success comes from hard work and being prepared for those opportunities that come your way.

-DOUG CLEMENS

Outfielder; St. Louis Cardinals, Chicago Cubs,
Philadelphia Phillies

My Best Day was meeting my wife and the days each of my 3 children were born.

My Best Day in Baseball was being a part of the 1964 Red Sox and the World Series.

Another Best Day was when the doctor told me that my cancer was treatable. I now have prostate cancer that is operable. God has a way of getting your attention!

-GEORGE THOMAS

Outfielder / Utility; Detroit Tigers, Los Angeles Angele, Boston Red Sox, Minnesota Twins

I had two at-bats when I got to St. Louis. I had just signed a bonus contract with them after I graduated from college. I hit both balls to the shortstop. I played in the minor league for an additional 4 years.

-JIM O'ROURKE
Pinch Hitter; St. Louis Cardinals

After reading your letter and learning of your surgeries and other health problems, I have come to the conclusion that today is my Best Day!

I am 81 years old and in reasonably good health (for someone my age). By comparison, there is no doubt that today has to be my Best Day.

-GUIDO GRILLI
Pitcher; Boston Red Sox, Kansas City Athletics

My Best Day moment is easy to remember. It was opening day at Dodger Stadium in 1964 and I got to play 3rd base in front of my mother & father. They were in the stands; my parents are my heroes and I owe everything to them.

-JOHN WERHAS
Third Baseman; Los Angeles Dodgers, California Angels

My Best Day was against the Milwaukee Braves in 1963.
Played against Lew Burdette and Warren Spahn. I went 6 for 8,
with two triples, 1 home run and 5 RBI's.

-AL MORAN

Short stop; New York Mets

Your story is remarkable and my Best Day, since there was only one, is nothing compared to your ordeal, but stay with it.

Another story may be of interest to you was a young guy (my father, Freddie Charles Linstrom) was born missing a lower back vertebra but became the youngest player to play in the World Series.

After playing on a Hall of Fame infield with the Giants, his back issue forced him to the outfield where he became a Hall of Fame outfielder with the Waner Brothers in Pittsburg.

-CHUCK LINSTROM
Catcher; Chicago White Sox, Perfect .1000 batting average

-FREDDIE LINDSTROM (Father)
Third Baseman / Outfielder; New York Giants, Pittsburgh Pirates, Chicago Cubs, Brooklyn Dodgers, National Baseball Hall of Fame, Youngest player (18) to play in a World Series (Giants)

After a desultory 1962 season in which I went from a blue-chip prospect to a suspect; I was sent to AA Augusta in 1963 and banished to the bullpen. The first 30 days I rarely pitched and when cutdown day came I was sent across the diamond to the opposing team. Their manager, Les Moss, asked if I could pitch that night because "you are all we got".

I pitched well for the first time in a year and then proceeded to win 15 regular season games with my 16th game in the playoffs.

Two years later I was in the Major Leagues with the Pittsburg Pirates. All because Les Moss said "you are all we got" and started me every four days after my previous owners let me rot in the bull pen.

PS: Did my fast ball get better walking across the diamond? Did my curve ball turn sharper? Did my control suddenly become pinpoint? What changed? MENTAL ATTITUDE.

-FRANK CARPIN
Pitcher; Pittsburgh Pirates, Houston Astros

I was a sandlot pitcher who worked my way up to the Major Leagues. Naturally, one of my Best Days was my first Major League win (as a Met) against the National Leagues leading Los Angeles Dodgers and Sandy Koufax

-DAV EILERS

Pitcher; Milwaukee Brave, New York Mets, Houston Astros

If I had played in an All-Star game or a World Series my Best Day would be easy for me.

I would have to say when I signed my first contract after graduation high school in 1955 is number one.

The day I hit two home runs in one game would be the other one. Finley Stadium had a fence put in right field exactly like Yankee Stadium, 296' down the line. The commissioner had them remove it after a few weeks.

-WAYNE CAUSEY
Infielder; Baltimore Orioles, Kansas City Athletics, Chicago White Sox, California Angels, Atlanta Braves

I've read your letter and it sent chills through my whole body. I've had some of them, but I'm lucky to still be able to play golf 3X a week. You must be some tough dude, keep hanging in there.

My most memorable day in the Majors was in Milwaukee. My dad, Jo-Jo White, was third base coach for Manager Bobby Bragen. It was the first game of the series, Braves against the Colt .45s. My mother was in attendance and bought her own ticket so she could sit behind the dugout.

We won the game and I went 4 for 4. I had a lot of sports writers asking questions after the game.

-MIKE WHITE
Center Field / Left Field; Houston Colt .45s / Astros

Amazing for someone who has been through all the trials you've had, to be centered on positiveness.

As a baseball player, my Best Day was in 1970. My dad, who had never seen me hit a homerun after high school, traveled to Cooperstown with me for the Exhibition Game between the Expos (my team) and the White Sox. Not only did he get to tour the Hall and meet many Hall of Famers, but he got to sit behind home plate at "Doubleday Field". I did not start the game, but went in at shortstop in the 4th inning. In my first at bat I hit one over the right field bleachers for my first homer since 1965. A friend of mine retrieved the ball,and gave it to my father. When I went out to play short stop the next inning, I saw dad holding that ball and kind of shifting it from hand to hand. I was filled with emotion to have given him that moment, and I think of it often. He passed away just 3 years later.

As far as life goes, today is my Best Day. I wake up next to my beautiful wife of 43 years. I am healthy, and I get to try to be better than yesterday. I am grateful to know that God lives, and that he hears my prayers and answers them in the way he knows is best for me.

-RON BRAND

Catcher; Pittsburgh Pirates, Houston Astros, Montreal Expos

I want to thank you for the opportunity to be a part of your upcoming book, but I can't pick out one Best Day in my life.

I have had so many Best Days it is not possible for me to pick one day that would be better than many others. God, family, sports; they have all been good. I have been blessed beyond my wildest dreams.

-RAY 'CORKY' WITHROW
Outfielder; St. Louis Cardinals

As a 21-year-old rookie third baseman playing for Detroit, my Best Day was during my second game in 1953. I went 3 for 5, scored a run. I only played one year in the Big Leagues, but it was the best.

-JOHN BAUMGARTNER

Third Baseman; Detroit Tigers

My Best Day is easy:

February 1st, 1958, when my wife and I were married. Though I had my share of sporting events, good days, this day tops all.

We have a family of seven children and now, eleven grandchildren. I couldn't be more thankful.

-JOHN DEMERIT
Milwaukee Braves, New York Mets, 1957 World Series Champion (Braves)

Per your request, I am sitting and pondering my Best Days.

As a professional baseball player, I pitched two one-hitters for the Hawaiian Islanders in 1965.

As an avid fisherman, it was catching a limit of speckled trout off the coast of North Carolina.

As a husband and father, it was standing over my first child, a daughter, in her crib.

As a grandfather, it was spending time with my two grandsons, Sawyer and Jackson.

As a Christian, it was turning my life over to Jesus Christ and His promise of eternal salvation.

-PETE CRAIG

Pitcher; Washington Senators

I was having a good year in AAA baseball, and I got called up, which was pretty unexpected. The guru's of baseball wanted me to stay and finish up my year in the minors, but Cardinals General Manager, Frankie Lane, decided differently. Frank met me at the St. Louis airport in his big, white Cadillac and he proceeded to tell me about all of the other pitchers, how they were doing and what they were doing wrong. Dixie Walker was my coach in AAA, and he gave me great advise. He said you know how to pitch, you got the call up, but the first thing they are going to try to do is change something that you do. Dixie told me to not pay attention to any of that, let it go in one ear and out the other ear. Sure enough, that is exactly what the pitching coach tried to do. They tried to change the way I grip the ball. I had to change to be able to pitch.

I got to pitch my first game 2 weeks later, against the Dodgers. 30,000 plus people in the stands, and I was scared to death. I pitched wild, and even gave up a home run in the 5th & 6th innings, and we lost. It was still quite an experience for a young boy.

-BOB BLAYLOCK
Pitcher; St. Louis Cardinals

347

My greatest moment in baseball happened on September 28th, 1963 when the Boston Red Sox played the Los Angeles Angels. With the score 3-2 in favor of the Angels, I came in to pitch in the top of the 7th. Dees doubled, Thomas walked and Torres came to the plate to sacrifice. He popped the ball up between the mound and 3rd base which it appeared I would catch easily. Torres just stood at home plate. Ed Bressoud, our Short stop, yelled to trap it. I did so and threw to Malzone at third, who threw Bressoud at 2nd, who threw Mantilla at first for an inning ending triple play. It was the last time I fielded a ball in the Big Leagues. I went on to pitch the 8th inning and struck out Perry; the last batter I faced in the Majors.

In my Major League debut in Detroit in 1962 I struck out Fernandez, their lead-off hitter; so I struck-out the first and last batters I faced in my brief Major League career. I believe I'm probably the only Major League player to start a triple play the last time they fielded a ball in the Big Leagues.

(I hope you can include my brief moment of fame in your book)

-PETE SMITH
Pitcher; Boston Red Sox

My Best Day was my 1960 debut. I pitched against Don Drysdale and the Los Angeles Dodgers in the LA Colosseum. We got beat, 2-0.

-JIM MALONEY

Pitcher, Cincinnati Reds, California Angels, 1965 All-Star, 2 no-hitters (1965, 1969) Cincinnati Reds Hall of Fame

My Best Day was October 6, 1962 when I married Jeri Smetak. She has been with me on this exciting baseball, business and retirement journey for fifty-eight years. Together we have raised three daughters and two grandchildren that have shared this wonderful life with us. We are truly blessed.

-LOU KLIMCHOCK

Infielder; Kansas City Athletics, Milwaukee Braves, Washington Senators, New York Mets, Cleveland Indians

You have quite a story- it makes my stroke and rotator cuff surgery seem trivial. You are right about a positive attitude; I know it has helped me. No "woes is me".

My Best Day was the day I made the Big Leagues and got a base hit on the first pitch thrown to me. Curt Simmons in St. Louis, September 1963.

-BILL COWAN
Outfielder; Chicago Cubs, New York Mets, Milwaukee Brewers, Philadelphia Phillies, New York Yankees, California Angels

My Best Day in life and in baseball was the Spring Day When manager Ralph Houk called me to the dugout in St. Petersburg, Florida to tell me I had won the James P. Dawson award giving to the outstanding rookie in camp and I was going to New York to start the season.

This was in 1961. I signed with the New York Yankees in June 1960 and after spending 3 days at the stadium, I was sent to Auburn, New York, Class D. The lowest rung of the minor leagues ladder. I had 15 wins, 1 loss and was invited to close out the year in New York. However, I was enrolled at UConn so I begged off to further my education. The General Manager, George Wiess, said Okay, we'll invite you to early spring training camp in 1961.

It all fell into place in 1961, with the expansion of the American League. The Yankees had to expose several players to the expansion team, Washington Senators and Los Angeles. I fit into the replacement system and Ralph Houk was eager to give a young player an opportunity.

-ROLLIE SHELDON

Pitcher; New York Yankees, Kansas City Athletics, Boston Red Sox; 1962 AL Pennant, 1962 World Series Champion (Yankees)

When I was 12 years old, I decided to play Little League in Norwood, Ohio. There was a rule that if you hadn't played Little League before you were 12, you couldn't pitch. So, I was a catcher. Our All-Star team made it to the State Finals against Masssilon. A ball was hit to right field with Mike Hershberger on third base. The throw came in, I caught it and turned, thinking a collision was coming, but Mike made a good slide under me and he was safe. We lost by 3.

Time went on and I got a basketball scholarship to the University of Cincinnati. I was on the same floor my freshman year with Mike Hershberger, who was there on a football scholarship. He dropped out of school his freshman year and I lost track of him.

In 1961 I signed with the "new" Washington Senators. As a pitcher I had a good rookie league record and was brought up to the "Bigs" in September. I was the only player to play on a National Championship Basketball Team and pitch in the Major Leagues in the same year, 1961. I spent a year at AAA in Syracuse, Johnny Van Der Meer was the manager, and in 1962 I was with Toronto AAA. I was brought up to the Senators in September of 1962 and got a start against the White Sox. In the 9th inning, we were leading 2-1 and the Sox had runners on 1st and 2nd, with 2 outs.

An announcement was made that a pinch hitter was coming in to bat: Mike Hershberger! I hadn't seen or heard of Mike for four years, and I sure didn't want him to ruin my win and complete game. He hit a 1-2 pitch on the ground to Ed Brinkman, who threw him out at first, so my Best Day in baseball was preserved. It turned out to be my only complete game in the "Bigs" and one of only 3 wins in my career. I tore my rotator cuff playing in Puerto Rico Winter Ball in 1964, so at 26 I was finished with baseball. So many good memories, though, so no regrets!

-CARL BOULDIN
Pitcher; Washington Senators

About the Author:

Mark Keys is a Southern California native, residing in Costa Mesa with his wife Laurie, daughters, Page and Megan, their dog, Fumble, and five cats, Lucy, Ethel, Sammy, Jack-Jack & George. Mark loves that his mom still lives at the beach in Newport in the house he grew up in, and he spends a lot of time there with her & the girls; and loves walking the beach. He played basketball growing up, in High School, and beyond; as well as body surfed until he injured his back. Mark is an avid reader, enjoys watching classic movies & westerns, collecting film and sports memorabilia, walking and listening to Jazz, Motown, and Rat Pack music. He also loves to travel and going to sporting events & team practices; when health permits. He also has started to design furniture. In spite of his numerous surgeries, including 6 back, 1 elbow (Tommy John Surgery) 15 ankle, 3 neck, 4 shoulder, and 11 knee surgeries (plus 4 knee replacements). He also experienced shingles, pneumonia, prostate infection, cancer, MRSA Staph infection. He lost his thyroid, testosterone and does not have an immune system. Neck surgery gave him a frozen vocal cord for half of a year. Mark fights continuous migraines and other health issues every day. But, through all of this, he keeps a positive attitude and outlook to make each day, his Best Day.

Made in the USA
Middletown, DE
06 September 2020

17980401R00199